To Kimberly,
I just met you but my feeling is that you are a sweet, giving spirit. May God continuously bless you; *Michael Elsa*

I dedicate this book to the memory
Of my mother,
Elsie Kathleen Johnson Jones
(May 5, 1936-November 11, 1980)
May you rest in peace.

Preface

This book is a journey that spans more than 30 years from its beginning, middle and end. It is like going from darkness, to dimness, to light in the span of a book. Writing it is a part of my purpose here on earth that God put on my heart long ago. It is my prayer that you, especially if you are lost, as I was, learn what it is to be transformed by the Hand of God. This is my journey, my testimony, my story. Minimally, I pray God uses this book to bless many to be able to see themselves in my experiences, on many levels, and to be able to walk away with something substantial that they didn't have or know before having read it. Maximally, I pray that his book changes lives and leads many to the Throne of Grace.

Part One is the first step in my journey, my quest for understanding in a confusing world. It was fully written and then copyrighted in June, 1984. I was 25 years old when it was completed. In this section I have not changed any context or ideas. The only changes that were made were done for clarity of what was being said or for structural reasons. So as you experience Part One remember I am 25. At the end of Part I, I thought I had "arrived", that I knew the truth.

Part Two I chronicles about an additional 25 years of my life, how I lived and how my life was. It covers drug addiction and all its deviants, and all my struggles and rewards. It ends with the real, permanent change.

Part Three Is a culmination. It answers the questions I had in Part 1, and reveals what God has taught me over the years and how my viewpoints and beliefs have changed. It is my transformation. It is the understanding that I yearned for long ago when I lacked understanding and sought the truth with a pure heart.

INSIDES OUT, PART 1, (THE BEGINNING-DARKNESS), Copyright 1984

To The Reader:

There was great turmoil going on my life when I experienced something that eventually brought me to oneness in spirit. Problems economically, dissatisfaction with society and lack of self-worth swarmed my head and I was brought to questioning the very essence and purpose for life; I also began to wonder if there was a reason for me to go on living. In that was a time that beckoned me to ask the metaphysical questions, "What is my purpose?", and "Does my purpose have an operation in physical or spiritual life?"

It was urgent for me to find my purpose and relate it to life, else I should not continue to suffer the injustice of the society that continued to condemn me, but take my life.

During the course of what I term "my experience", many of what I consider "revelations" came to me that placed me in a realm of philosophical knowledge and gave me a peace of mind. From this realm of philosophical knowledge, I understood my purpose, which will be expressed in this book. I would like to declare that any new opinions or concepts expressed in this book are exclusively my own and that, being such, they are to be related to you as a possible foundation to build your philosophy upon, not as factual formula.

It was my purpose to write this book to show you that "the Spirit of God dwells in you" and that the possibility exists that you may not fully grasp the truth unless you give your mind to The Creator so that He might show you the truth. My words are to touch upon your empirical experiences and to bring into understanding as many concepts as possible to mix with concepts you may have in a fragmented understanding of universal purpose.

This book is a transformation from a standard way of thinking into thought guided by my perception and God's grace. (1984)

The Manifestation of a Dream

Looking upon the powers of my inner self,
Seeking the positivism to relieve myself
Of the bondage I felt within my spirit,
I became the manifestation of what I believed
Would free me from the grasp of what I had been taught was real.

Adapting my thought to
The rules I applied to my mind,
I became the lone member
Of a cult of my own construction.

Limited to my philosophy of self,
I was unable to conceive an orthodox means
Of communication.

I could not be understood,
But I always knew what I meant and felt.
And very seldom did I use words t relate,
Because expressions seemed more effective.

Because of what I adapted as symbology,
I was often confused by what I saw,
But not my analogy of what was happening.

I was free in mind and spirit
In a world that knew nothing of it.
The realities of this civilization
Did not exist in my organization of thought,
And I was aware that they believed
I was mad.

I laughed at them because they were
Not aware that I was the wisest of all.
I was one of the goddesses of earth
Because I had overcome all that is.
I had risen above the conception of life
That I had been taught.

In time I realized that I would not be allowed
To survive freely in the world.
I was forced to awaken
From this manifestation of my dream   --Michelle Elaine (1984)

PART ONE—DARKNESS

Chapter 1: My philosophy
(1979)

"Ah, I'm so glad it's 4 o'clock," I said as I changed clothes to go home. It had been a long day doing my normal routine at the cafe within the law firm. I had not been to sleep until about 3:00 that morning and had to get up at 5:00 to come to work. I could remember getting up and washing my face that morning so that I could see the toilet clearly enough to know if the rim was down. When I got washed up, I went into our room and woke Stella up. She had her head at the edge of the bed by the end table and already in position to put her hands directly on her cigarettes when she opened her eyes. She sat up, lit a cigarette, positioned herself like the "The Thinker", then shook her head and aimed toward the bathroom with a nasty disposition, as usual. When she came out, I was dressed and she was ready to at least say "Morning".

We continued to ready ourselves, then left the apartment for work. When we got outside, I remembered b that I did not have my 80 cents change to catch the bus.

"Stella, give me change for a dollar."

."Oh, hell, now I gotta dig down in 'his shit". She looked as though she was agitated as she searched for the change. Man, she was not a morning person. "Gimme the dollar! I'm gon' start charging' your ass for getting my change all the time."

"No you won't"

"Well how 'bout I'll beat your ass, then." I just laughed.

She always told me that. We were getting on the bus and she put the money in. I said, "You better gimme my 20 cents" as we headed to the bus.
"You ain't getting' nothin' 'less u beat my ass."

"That's possible." We looked around and discovered that woke up everybody on the bus, so we just sat down quietly. Stacy sat across the aisle on the seat parallel to mine and gave 'the eye' and I made a face at her. By that time we had reached the next stop. About 5 people got on the bus. We always noticed the girl who stood about 5'4, 250 pounds. She wore a big blue wool coat, a super-thick wool scarf, lumberjack boots, and wore what looked like the same jeans every day. She carried with her two stuffed canvas bags, and a big striped umbrella. She had a plain pale face and shaggy looking hair. Every morning she took a little purse out of her jeans pocket, showed her flash pass, sat in her seat, then raised her bottom high enough to stuff the purse back in her jeans and sat down again, crushing whoever she sat beside, not even saying excuse me. Nobody wanted her to sit by him and would sometimes compromise and sit together to avoid sitting by her. By the time she was settled, I was almost asleep. I woke up when we reached our subway stop. We put our cards through the gate just as we heard the train our coming.

"Michelle, hurry up and change, Toni is taking us home and it's almost 4:15."
"I'm going over Teddy's"
"Okay, I'll see you tomorrow."

I left the building and caught the bus up 16th Street to Teddy's house. I liked his neighborhood because it had a nice atmosphere and I felt safe there. I walked two blocks down and got the food I would prepare for tonight's dinner.

When I got to the apartment, I said to myself "Same old apartment." It was an old building with high ceilings. The apartment had four rooms. The living room was really a bedroom, cluttered with things Teddy had thrown around within the last few days. I sat the groceries in the kitchen and began making the bed and hanging the clothes, just making the first room entered a little more presentable. After I straightened up the kitchen, I lit a joint that I had brought from a New York 'refa hole'. It was laced with PCP (angel dust). I was cooking and I thought about a little red composition notebook I had been writing in. I started writing in it after I read a part of a book, which spoke of the power of attaining the things one desires.

When I did not finish the book (since I could not find it), I reached my own conclusions of how to acquire the power of my desire. I believed that a certain universal truth existed to be related to people and that if I could find it, I could share it with others and bring about a universal peace.

But how could I find this truth? First I had to start with myself. What were the reasons I was not spiritually and physically at peace? I knew I had to admit my insecurities, explore my possibilities, and learn to believe in myself. This was a necessary reflection because I realized that peace must start somewhere and that I could never communicate truth unless I had peace within the realm of what I believed.

I was cutting up the potatoes to boil while I asked myself questions aloud and began to answer them aloud. The answers sounded like answers I would give to any person who asked me the same questions, so I concluded that I was not being completely honest with myself. I began to use word association with myself to get more deeply into what my problems were; I realized that the way I truly felt inside was buried so deeply beneath norms and social mores that I no longer knew the reality of my own mind and spirit. My problems or "hang-ups" were of guilt, fear, I felt I was not attractive, and I lacked confidence in myself. Therefore, I would never completely communicate the truth as I should as long as I remained in this state.

I put the potatoes in water to boil and sat the pan on the stove. I plugged the radio in by the bed and sat at the table. Then I continued to concentrate trying to touch upon the reason I could not get fully into my own deep feelings. Word association did not satisfy my wants, nor did concentrating. I thought it was a shame that I did not even know myself, and I was all the more determined to discover my true self.

Then I remembered the 'Id', 'the ego' and the 'super ego' from Freudian psychology. Each represented different members of a single personality. I figured there were at least 3 components to my personality, then. I named them 'me', 'myself' and I. 'Me' was the same as the child in me, 'myself' was the component of my personality which weighed situations and made judgements, and 'I' was the supreme judge of all opinion and could override 'me' and 'myself'. 'I' would be responsible for writing the law by which I would live, which would be termed My Philosophy. All other concepts of character and thought would be under the law, which would be created by in depth reflection into self. It was only through honest interpretation of logical "sense" information that would come from within, that I could finally state and obey the laws of mind. This would be my democracy. And I could trust it as it had come from me and no outside influence.

Times that I wrote and practiced my philosophy was divided into segments of days when I visited Teddy and had time alone to do so. The law would be a set standard which I could surrender my mind to and operate within to gain spiritual insight, which I believed would be revealed to me when they were complete. The law was a declaration of my spirit and my convictions, which I would mentally reveal to the world of spirit as a foundation to reveal to me through. By making my declaration, I felt that what I truly sought (the truth) would be revealed to me in the spirit that I asked that it be. The laws. Would be used to fashion my ways of thinking, to mold my mind for the truth. So they would be memorized and consciously obeyed.

Chapter 2, The Law

I started writing in the red composition notebook with the first of the laws of my philosophy: 1) I AM NOT PERFECT. In that I declaring that the 'I' of my personality could not be absolutely right at all times, but was the judge that ruled 'me' and 'myself'. All other laws would be written under that principle that the 'I' was ruler by hierarchical structure, but was not infallible. The 'I' would listen to all thoughts as I meditated and sift through those thoughts not pertinent to discovery of my true self, eliminate them and write only laws which would govern me and my actions.

2) FIRST I MUST BE MYSELF, THEN I CAN DO THE OTHER THINGS THAT I WANT TO BE A PART OF ME. Here was the law which would govern my career. I felt that I should be what I thought was really me, and that would determine my career. I loved to write but lacked the confidence to make writing my career. I concluded that I had to be truly myself (when I discovered what that was) and then I could choose my career.

3) TO ME, WHAT EXISTS IS; WHAT DOES NOT EXIST DOES NOT. Here I questioned the existence of God. I made an agreement with God in what I believed to be my last prayer: "I have heard word of your existence and I have read of your existence. Man wrote those books, and in time he will change them to control the masses of people around the world and to benefit those in power as much as possible. You have not shown me that You exist. If I am wrong, You know haw this thought came to be. If this is the greatest sin I have

ever committed, I will know when You show me that You really do exist and that You hold the truth".

About that time Joe, Teddy's roommate came in. We talked for a few minutes then I find wished cooking the meal. Joe left before I finished and before Teddy got home. since I was bored with the television, I went back to writing the laws of my philosophy.

4) ONE WAY THAT IAM IS THAT I FEEL EMOTIONS ALONG WITH THE DEALINGS OF THE MIND. It was obvious that the formulation of my philosophy would begin to separate the relationship that Teddy and I shared. One thing Teddy cared nothing about was the details of other people's characters. He was only interested to the degree that was necessary to relate well with them on whatever basis the situation demanded. I would not adopt his attitude and would allow room for emotion and feeling as it related to the formulation of my philosophy of my character.

5) MY MIND IS MY MOTIVATION TO LEARN. Never before had I wanted to learn for myself, as opposed to being spoon-fed what I should learn and being forced to swallow. Knowledge now meant that I would be able to voice my opinions on as many subjects as I would learn about or have a general mental concept of and my opinion now mattered.

6) I AM NOT A WRITER, I AM A PHILOSOPHER BECAUSE PHILOSOPHY IS OPINION AND THAT IS WHAT I WRITE. As I wrote, my philosophy became fact for me. The way that the 'I' saw things became the way they were, and nothing could change the facts of "My Philosophy" because my opinion (philosophy) was just as valid as anyone else's.

7) I WILL BELIEVE WHAT I BELIEVE UNTIL I BELIEVE DIFFERENTLY. I would determine the reality of all things and believe how they seemed to me. That was because I got a certain tranquility from being and doing what I thought I should do, think or be. Any event of change would not come to be unless there was also a change in my overall philosophical viewpoints, which would precipitate change of a law.

8) MY OPINION IS ANOTHER WAY OF SAYING HOW I FEEL. Formulating my own philosophy would also allow me to express my feelings of love which would also become conceptual in nature.

There were there tangible items of today's modern society which I had yet to fully grasp in order to have happiness in the world. I felt I had a weight problem, which was the major reason I had anxieties; money problems; and career problems. Success seemed a thing of a past, which I never knew. I had to do something to help the world to see that the world's goal should not be to make the dollar, but to live and work together, giving to one another, that no one should have to do without necessities, but to gain by his efforts to uplift the spirit of humankind.

In order to determine what courses would be the right ones to take in hypothetical situations, in which I guessed what movements were necessary to set the stage for revelations of truth and expose any counterparts of the revelations of truth, I determined that there three ways of viewing a given situation: from a negative standpoint, from a positive standpoint or from an altogether different standpoint from my personality components, 'me', 'myself' and 'I'. Of course, 'I' would have the last word.

Soon Teddy came home. He banged on the door like a maniac, as usual. That would always start our 'play fights' and end hugs and kisses. As Teddy ate, I wanted to tell him everything on my mind, but somehow, I couldn't. I guess I was afraid of the way I felt about him, afraid of losing him, and because I had never wanted anything as much as his love. I believed that if I told him I would destroy every chance I had of receiving all of his love for mine: That would be crossing that forbidden turf between his feelings and his freedom. I knew he cared, but I knew that was all to it. I had to keep telling myself not to push it until the time was right.

The next morning, I woke up before the clock went off. It was so hot in the room. I could only see the limbs of a tree as I looked out of the window and into the darkness. I made a gesture to turn the heat off and the banging pipes of the radiator. Teddy stirred and drew me close to him. I decided to enjoy his warmth for the last time before we went to work.

The next time I woke up, the sun was coming up and I knew I was late. It was 7:00.

"Get up, Teddy, It's late."

"What time is it?"

It's seven o'clock".

I started pressing clothes and Teddy went for the bathroom.
"You got anything you want me to iron?"

"Get that brown shirt out of the closet."

After I finished ironing, I looked at the time.
Damn, it's 7:15. Stella's gon' be mad as hell."

I rushed and washed up. All the while, I was thinking about the little book and about what my actions might be at work. I got dressed and, as usual, I had to wait for Teddy to pack his little airline bag that he took to work every day.

"You ready?", he asked.

"Soon as I get my coat on."

The radio said it was 7:25. At 7:31 I was late, so I decided that it was too late to rush. I remembered that Lois would be taking Teresa's place as I walked down the hall of the cafe. When I opened the door, I caught Stella's eye. She looked as though she was saying "You know you're 15 minutes late. You know we have to play the role. So..." I took off my hat and coat and threw them on top of the coffee boxes stacked by the wall behind the counter. Stella said "You might as well put your coat back on because you have to help Judy carry her stuff (foods) to the other building."

"Shouldn't I wait for the bread man."

"Yes, wait for the bread man", she said in an aggravated tone. I had to give her credit. She's a very good actress. She continued, "You

14

getting' docked for being late, you getting' fired if you keep begin' late."

"I already know that, Stella. So I'll try to get up earlier."

"Try?"

"Okay, I will get up earlier," I laughed.

"Ain't nothing funny".

"Stella, you wanna know why I'm late?"

"I don't what to hear your stories. Just make sure you don't fall behind in coffee or nothing' else."

By that time Judy was packed up to go to the other building.

"You all have a nice day. I'll see you later", Judy said.

I poured a cup of coffee and put two packets of sugar and a packet of cream in it. I ate a donut while I waited for the bread man.

As the bread man entered the door. I was finishing my coffee. I started putting my coat on. When I was bundled up, I packed Judy's bread in the box with other foods she would need for the day. I put my keys and the joint of marijuana Teddy had given me in my pocket, then I started out the door with the box. I hummed to myself and I walked over to the other part of the law firm in another building through the back of the main building. The building was across the street on another block. I left Judy's box and rushed outside to smoke the joint while I walked around the park. "That was nice," I said to myself as I reentered the building for work once again.
I changed into my uniform and started to work. I watched people's faces as they dragged in for that first cup of coffee. I made myself busy by stacking coffee filters and coffee from packets in stacks of six. I started thinking about the night before as I poured water into the top of the coffee maker.

In line with the thought that there was divine purpose in human life, I arrived at the conclusion that there was a reason for every thought or train of thought. I decided that any of my logic must lead to a certain law then return full circle to its point of origination in order to organically function with the law. I realized that my philosophy was too limited because its laws didn't cover everything in order for my organic functions to exist and to function as a system. So I had to expand my philosophy and expand myself.

For the rest of that morning, I only stopped thinking to say "good morning" to people as they came in. I finished making the cottage cheese and fruit containers and loaded them into the vending machine. As I started my huge salad that sat inside the salad bar I thought. I particularly remembered some of the trains of thought I indulged in that day. These "trains" of thought were like monologues in my mind:

"Okay. What I want to do is expand my mind. I need something to start with. Beliefs--I'll start with beliefs. Before last night, my strongest belief was God. What's wrong with God? For one thing, I can't agree with the concept of God and Christ. Somehow it doesn't fit because people are enslaved by it. The only people with power seem not to have the same concepts that were taught to me. There must be certain knowledge of God that some men know, but will not reveal to the masses of people. Why? Because everyone would have the ultimate power if they should reveal the secret. What power? Whatever power there is that gives power itself. Energy? Not physical power because all men are mortal. No, this power is invisible and it is like strength within spirit. It is not violent--it is an inevitable wisdom and truth combined. What can be judged from this? I am my truth and I believe that of the words given in my realm of knowledge, God will remain in question. Before I bar the possibility of God, I must research the books that give any certain truth. Bibles must not have a part in the consideration of the reality or non-reality of God. I needed to come to grips with the literature of ancient times to find what might have been lost in the interpretations of our present day. I must also study evolution. At this point I must say overall that I must not force a belief in God without research. Why is the concept God the strongest belief of self? It is my belief that I exist and that God possibly exists.

Is man from God's creation or did man create God. Did the earth form from energy of space with its stars, or from the molding of God's hands? Did evolution precede God or did God foresee evolution? All of these are questions we must consider in research. This is the greatest question of self because it is the question of existence itself. How could we be sure that man will give us the truth of God? We would receive the truth only as well as man has known it, and to extent that man has known it. We are not to try and deface God, but to realize the fact that He does or does not exist. Why do we give God a sex? I do not like the repetition of "He". If God is spirit there is no sex. If God existed, I believed that God must reveal the truth to the eyes of those who seek him with urgency and truthfulness, and without fear of man-made morals. Is it safe to assume that man is his own God--just possibly? If man lives in spirit after death, it may be possible for a man to be his own God, to be his own existence, choosing his own next form of life after death, placing his spirit in the object that he chooses."

I looked at the clock and it was 10:37. I had started the chili and begun placing it in large and small serving cups. I had one more can to fix, and I had one can of soup left to make. I had to fill the coffee urn, too. Lois looked at me while I poured some chili in the container at my station. You've been awfully quiet today", she said.

"I'm just trying to sort some things out", I said. I went on with my work, then I sat at one of the tables close to the television with a scoop of egg salad, crackers, and some apple juice. It was 11:00 and "All in the Family" was coming on. I was not very hungry, but I ate anyway. Just after I finished and was trying to watch television, Teddy sneaked up behind me and stuck a finger in my ear, knowing how sensitive I was to his doing so. I pinched him. He rubbed his leg and went over to the phone near the television. When he got off of the phone, he assured me that he would be getting me back later on. I just laughed.

All in the family had gone off and I decided to change the "day special" board from beef stew to chili. I took the frame off the wall and placed it on the table to change the letters. I rang up the money on the side of the register. (Customers would leave their coffee money on the side of the register rather than disturb us when we were busy.) After I finished changing the letters, Stella asked me to go to get the cash box from the safe on the fifth floor. I put the money in the register and put the box behind the counter. I opened the vending machine and emptied its metal box on the table. I counted $48.45. I wrapped what would not fit in the register drawer slots. A few more people came in and I rang up their food then sat at a table and watched the 12:00 soap opera. Lois came from behind the counter.

"What's happenin'?", she asked.
"Jill is on her way to Mr. Brooks to get married."
"Where is Derek."
"He's on his way back from seeing his son at the hospital. He just thought about meeting Jill."

About half way through the show, people really started pouring in and I had to run the register too often to enjoy the rest of the show. Lois had to start making sandwich orders and Stella serviced my section.

By 1:00, the tables were filled with secretaries watching "All My Children". By 1:30, the line had thinned out to a few straggling customers, and I was a le to think without too many interruptions.

I realized I had not decided on a slogan or symbol for my internal government, known as my philosophy. I tried to figure out a slogan from what I had formulated so far. It would be a perfect representation of my philosophy. I also realized that there was not a lot of cohesiveness in my philosophy yet because the laws that operated my philosophy were not complete. Thinking about that fact, I came up with the slogan:

IF IT DON'T FIT DON'T FORCE IT. Since I would live by the perceptions of my three persons, 'me', myself, and 'I', and since I would always allow three other viewpoints for consideration by my three persons (a positive, negative and a neutral additional viewpoint). I then worked on my symbol. I chose the number 3, for 'me', 'myself' and 'I'. Then I choose the pyramid as a symbol as well, to represent the knowledge of ancient times. So, the complete symbol became a pyramid with the number 3 on one side, inside of a perfect circle.

By the time I chose my symbol, it was time to clean up for the day. I left the register and resumed my usual tasks talking to Lois instead of thinking of my philosophy.

After we had cleaned up, Lois and I went and sat at the table to the left of the television. I decided to call Teddy and see what the plans would be for the evening. I dialed the number and it rang twice. I talked to Teddy. He had some things to take care of, so I decided to go back over my Aunt Stella's house for the night.

After Stella and I got off the bus at our usual stop, we walked to the liquor store to pick up our daily sip. I had to give her credit; she took care of her business at work, did her required paperwork at home, cooked dinner sometimes (when Gregory, her son didn't) continued to do jigsaw or crossword puzzles then started watching television before she took that first wind-down sip.

As we walked in the door of the liquor store, I saw the same black man that I usually saw. He was handsome and had a slightly chubby body that made him almost boyishly cute. He had been used to seeing us both come in the door together, but lately I had begun to visit Teddy. The man called me and Stella 'Stuff 1 and Stuff 2. I was Stuff 2. He did a double take then asked me, "So where you been?

I didn't reply. I just grinned.
He said, "I heard you been spending time 'cross town"

"Who is your source?"

"Well now, I can't go 'round giving up my sources. Ain't that uh, snitchin'?"

"OK, then I don't have to comment."

"Ok. Ima let you go this time. Lucky I want to keep seeing y'all 'round here. but if you ever want to adopt a daddy..."

"The one I have is quite enough. I'm glad to be away from him." We all laughed.

We always played around like that. My mind was somewhere that day. When we got to the apartment, I opened a beer and talked to Stella for a while. Then I watched television for a while. I watched television for a while, and tired of that, then I listened to the radio. I sat on the bed and thought about some of the laws of my philosophy. I could not be bored with that.

I tried to think of more laws that I should add to it. So far, with repetition, the laws of self that I elected to obey were just beginning to change me. They changed what I let into my scope. This was a good thing because my thoughts had been extremely positive and in had no regrets about anything I did. I had no conscience, unless it happened to be my philosophy, so I felt no guilt, because my laws were totally me. I felt a great urge to express my thoughts and my laws to people. I laid on the bed in quiet thought, debating whether certain laws should be added to my philosophy, based upon laws that were already a part of my philosophy.

The next day, I was preoccupied with thoughts about what laws I should add to my philosophy. Once I caught myself speaking aloud. Lois heard me and asked me what I was talking about. I thought all day and before I knew it, the day was over. Evidently I performed my duties to Stella's satisfaction, though I only vaguely remembered performing them.

I called Teddy and he came up to bring me his key. When I got into his apartment, I straightened things up before going to the store. I reached for my coat and remembered the joint in my pocket. I smoked it and bundled up, then left for the store.

I felt very light and free-spirited as I walked up the street. The winter's breeze felt good on my face.

In the store, I smiled and greeted everyone who passed by me. I chose the foods I needed very carefully. I was still smiling when I left the store. It felt good to have time to myself to think about what I considered important. It gave me a sense of self-worth and gave me time to let go of some of the problems of society's oppression which hovered over me. For once I would see some pleasure in my life. For once I would not let my problems deny me the joy of my own inner beauty. I could not wait to start writing some more of my philosophy.

As soon as I had taken my coat off in the apartment, I seasoned the cubed steak and turned the heat down under the pan. After the butter melted, I put the steak in the pan and peeled some potatoes. After everything was cooking at a moderate temperature, I headed for the book.

9) MY SECRET TO RELEASING SELFISHNESS IS REALIZING THAT I NEVER KNOW ANYTHING. I believed that a person who thought he always knew everything was not only limiting himself, but also was selfishly preventing his mental expansion. I would never be the type to say I KNOW anything but one who expresses an opinion of knowledge as I saw, understood or remembered it. To me, words were limited in their ability to express, so there was no complete knowledge of fact other than self. It was only important to realize that everything was possible.

10) MY PHILOSOPHY CAN NEVER BE USED AS FACT, SO I DO NOT STATE IT TO BE. It was only fact for me.

11) I BELJEVE THAT HE WHO SEEMS WISE IS ONLY AWARE OF THE MIND'S FUNCTIONS. The awareness of some functions of the mind was held back from the masses and that was the reason for our "false culture" and the reason we didn't have the truth.

12) I SHOULD LEARN ALL THAT I CAN FROM THE OPINIONS OF OTHERS AND CREATE MY OWN OPINIONS FROM WHAT I LEARN. First fact became philosophy, then philosophy became opinion. I allowed three terms to represent knowledge: fact (of self), philosophy (of self and life), and opinion(of both fact and philosophy). It would be my duty to listen to all opinions about a certain subject, then decide what, if anything, should be added to complete the concept of the law of my philosophy.

I was aware that a lot of the meanings of lost ancient words which spoke of wisdom had been lost in translation. The loss was in the terms used to describe the derivative of each word. It was the loss of wisdom as it could no longer be completely accessed. It became necessary to write the law of self which would ward off the possibility of that happening when I communicated my philosophy.

13) I BELIEVE THAT THE MORE COMPLICATED A WORD IS, THE MORE DISTANCE THERE IS IN COMMUNICATION. The average person was not a high scholar, and I wanted my work to speak to the masses, ultimately. So I would keep it simple so mostly everyone would understand what my philosophy was about; so I wouldn't lose people because they couldn't understand the words.

14) I DO NOT BELIEVE I CAN HAVE A SERIOUS FIGHT BECAUSE I AM NOT SERIOUS WHEN I AM FIGHTING. There was only one way to look at a fight--as violence at one level-- physical punishment of an immediately painful type. I was thinking of the struggles of our leaders who had either died or been assassinated, Nonviolence got across, but violence did not. It accomplished nothing, and I wondered why the fighting, as useless as it was, became the way to conquer as opposed to negotiation and compromise.

15) I WILL REMEMBER WHAT I BELIEVE IN BECAUSE I WILL BELIEVE IN WHAT I REMEMBER. I began to wonder if I might someday lose sight of my philosophy, so I drew this conclusion. I had many different thoughts and reviewed many concepts during the past week or so, as I developed my philosophy. It was impossible to to keep track of them all. However, I concluded that anything that was welcomed or made sense in my philosophy would be automaticly obeyed when my philosophy was in operation.

16) DEFINATION IS OPINIONATED, SO I DON'T ACCEPT IT AS FACT. It was definition and the concepts associated with words that controlled people's thoughts and minds. If definitions or concepts associated with words were incorrect or misleading, the truth might never be known. Even one might read something and misinterpret it or see something his own eyes, and still misinterpret what he sees.

In about an hour, Teddy's frantic knock called me to the door again. I let him in and went into the kitchen to warm the food. I looked in to the living room and watched Teddy undo his tie. I smiled at him.

I continued to write as Teddy ate and watched television.

17) I BELIEVE SCIENCE FICTION IS THE BEST TYPE OF MEDIA, BECAUSE WHAT IT SAYS, IN ESSENCE, IS THAT ANYTHING IS POSSIBLE. There was reason to be concerned with the media because the media had the job of telling the truth. Well, I could see that the media read so much into situations that the situations changed before they became news. Science fiction was already fiction so it couldn't be corrupted or compromised in society. That's because they were not real, either.

18) I BELIEVE IN THE GOOD OF ALL PEOPLE. I believed that all people were good before being influenced by the media and the opinions of others around them, who caused them to form the same negative and narrow-minded beliefs. I also believed that deep down, in all people, was a good person, even though their goodness may not have been externally demonstrated yet.

19) I BELIEVE THE WORLD WAS BETTER BEFORE IT WAS INFLUENCED. This law was derived from thoughts about influences that made the masses of people believe that they should form concrete images of intangible things. I was speaking of governments worldwide, which dictated what the people should have to be complete, then they dictated how they should have it; they dictated specific principles of the real and unreal, seen and unseen, right and wrong, law and order, failure and success, and convinced the people that theirs was the natural order of things. It was because of that that the people, one of whom I was, ending up not knowing ourselves or the truth.

20) I DON'T BELIEVE IN RIGHT OR WRONG. I believed that a judgement could be right and wrong depending on the situation and the individual's sense of right and wrong, for there was no absolute right or wrong.

21. I BELIEVE I SHOULD SAY WHAT'S ON MY MIND BUT KNOW WHY IM SAYING IT.

Knowing that language was limited, I knew that words used to express any idea, sentiment, emotion, assertion, had to be wisely chosen, and that unless the words spoken could be used to help enlighten others, they should not be spoken.

I put the book down and Teddy asked me to come and sit with him in the chair. As we watched television I thought of some times in the past when I made ridiculous mistakes and I hung my head in shame. I told myself not to dwell on the past. However, I did not quite know why I had had the thoughts that suddenly swept across my mind.

In about an hour, Teddy had fallen asleep in the chair. I kept nudging and calling him until he was awake. After I got Teddy dressed for bed, I got myself dressed for bed. It took a while to go to sleep, but when I did, I slept soundly.

The next night, I stayed at Stella's apartment. She told me she had a date that evening. She kept asking me if I would be okay. I didn't know why she asked, but I kept telling her I would be fine. She had told me a few days before that she had had to be high to talk to me lately. I wondered if what I said to her over the past week was beyond her reach or if it was beyond reason. I decided to 'believe what I believed until I believed differently'. If I came to believe differently, I would change my philosophy.

Several days passed and nothing more than the reinforcement of my laws in my mind was important to me. However, on Monday, January 29, 1979, I decided that the following few days would tell the story of the actual way of the world. I was going to determine the way of the world by being negative one day, being positive one day, and being neutral one day, as an individual. This way I could determine the general mood of the people in the world. I would have to understand the peoples' moods (general) in relation to the events and practices of law and religion in this country.

Chapter 3
"Three Shades of Life"

Monday, January 29 1979

     I woke up before the clock went off. It was very dark outside. I pushed the alarm in and noted the time. It was 4:30 a.m. I turned the light on and lit one of Stacy's cigarettes. I had not smoked one for a while because I was trying to quit. I smoked a joint and went to the bathroom and took a shower.

When I got to work, I performed my duties well but quietly. All day I quietly repeated my laws in the privacy of my mind: "I am not perfect. First I must be myself, then I can do the other things that I want to be a part of me. To me what exists is and what does not exist, isn't. This is a part of my mind. I must feel emotions along with the dealings of the mind. My mind is my motivation to learn. I will believe what I believe until I believe differently. This is a part of my mind, this is a part of myself. I must remember to realize that I never really <u>Know</u> anything. My philosophy is not fact, so I must not state it to be. I should learn all I can from opinions of others and create my own opinions from what I learn. This is a part of my mind, this is a part of the unity of my inner self…"
     Gradually, I began to think in patterns and it became more apparent that this meditation altered my behavior, thoughts, responses and feelings.

     I prepared the coffee and wrapped cakes and donuts as usual. I thought about how I had planned to be completely positive today and I would be positive. Judy was doing her usual weighing of meats and cheeses. I watched her as she nervously smoked her cigarette whenever she paused a moment. She seemed to be afraid of Stella all of the time. But I never got any breaks by working with my Aunt and I did not think she should either; if she had trouble doing her job, which was not difficult, that was her problem. All that Stella ever asked was that we used common sense and got our jobs done. She also suggested that common sense would in some cases make jobs easier if it was utilized. I thought Judy was just a nervous sort of person.

Anyway, nothing was going to destroy the day for me. As people began to pour in for pastries, toast and coffee, I kept making more coffee, setting up my station in between. Somehow I managed not to run out of coffee that day.

I was very enthusiastic and I voluntarily helped people with money stuck in machines and other minor problems that Stella was just too busy to be bothered with. She had a lot of paperwork and those minor problems interrupted her. I even stopped eating lunch to cooperate with and help people when I did not have to. I was very pleasant and I seemed to cheer people up. Between my deeds, I repeated my laws the whole day through.

Teddy came upstairs slightly before 4:00 and gave me the key to the apartment.
He said he would be in around 8:00.

When I got to the apartment, I cleaned up the usual wreck, then I went to the store and put the food on the stove for the evening.

I got my red tablet out and began reading over my philosophy again. It was so important for my subconscious mind to get ample doses of it so that it could be molded into my character. I would reinforce it as much as I could because I would be the supreme example of the communication I would give to others—the power of the mind individually and the power of the masses of minds combined to bring forth a happier more peaceful nature in people. Most of all, I would try to communicate a method to acquire world peace. My philosophy would be my beginning. When others saw the difference in me, they would also want to see that kind of difference for themselves. That would be a second step towards a greater end.

Tuesday, January 30, 1979

Today, as I prepared for the usual crowd, I came to the realization that this would be my negative day. But I should in no obvious way be totally negative. I should instead, make calm, but negative responses to statements to those who made negative statements to me. At other times, I would be quiet.

And so I did perform in my negative way and I had gotten many responses.

I searched for a word that day. A word connected with nationwide communication be it within music, art, or literature. I wanted a word that the young (adolescents) were already using to communicate. Something I could present to them in a greater light than the level than they presently identified with it.

I thought for a while. I know one thing, they were surely into music. But what one concept do they really get into? Oh, of course. The word with the young is "funk". Funk was a concept created in trying to express the mood of the music they listened to, as was the word "bad" was a concept relating to how nice something really was. I wondered why people to used words, to mean what could be described it as their opposite. Maybe that was how society was: the opposite of what it was supposed to be.

When I could not think of a concept to relate directly with funk, I determined that "funk" had to be the concept: funk had to be the means through which the idea of world peace should be expressed. When I thought of the concept of world peace, I knew a formula should be devised to bring the concept into reality. I did not as yet know how I would come up with the formula, but I knew I would find it in my meditations. I knew people would listen if I called it funk.

Wednesday, January 31, 1979

I allowed this day to pass before I had my neutral day. I also allowed the next day to pass before my neutral day. The time was used to understand the ways of people as experienced by two different attitudes but the same individual. I took note that when I was positive and cooperated with the people who came into the café, my effort was appreciated, but was appreciated in a way that showed me that my attitude should be the same way every day--positive, regardless to personal feelings. When I was negative and would not cooperate, there was much friction and people seemed to be watching me, possibly wondering if I would again say something to make it understood that my only goal for the day was to do only what was necessary to perform my job successfully, nothing more. I wondered why I was noticed more when I was uncooperative than I was when I was exceptionally cooperative.

There was a good in all people; a good that they did not have to realize and a good that could not help coming out in all they did, for it was the inner self. They had to be reached before they could ever know that. Tonight I would try to think of a nationally universal way to express the messages I had to express to others.

I could not come up with a way to express the messages I had to express. But there had to be a way. I knew that what I sought, I sought honestly and truthfully. I hoped that through my honest, pure thoughts, I would come about the absolute and indisputable truth. "There must be a way", I said to myself. Was there a road or clues to follow? I asked the power of my mind to show me the path, give me the insight to interpret the signs along the way, and prepare me for each phase of pure enlightenment.

Thursday evening, I thought more about the subject. I wondered why God had not shown me the light of truth and the answer of why the world was as it was. There were three possible reasons that God had not shown me the things I wanted to know (that is, if he existed). God could have been waiting for the people of earth to destroy themselves; He could be waiting until a particular time to relieve everyone from their troubles and take us all unto him; He could be willing to teach us as we walked the path of the search for Him and the truth He held. Would He at least show me the path? Did He exist?

Friday, February 2, 1979
Today I was to act neutrally when I was in contact with people. I was to be neither positive nor negative. I was just supposed to act with common sense, but not let my attitude toward peoples' actions be noticeably positive or negative.

I got no responses from others when I acted in this manner. I would not speak unless spoken to, and I simply said as little as possible. I was not unpleasant, but I was not pleasant either. I did not make jokes and I did not participate in conversations with others. I did not laugh at jokes but I did engage in opportunities to take advantage of automatically negative attitudes of some automatically negative people who were patrons of the cafe.

I got no responses, no irregularities in peoples' reactions to me when I had a neutral attitude when I did my work and interacted with them early that day. So, people in society, based on my experience of the past few days, told me that at least the people in the firm were more neutral than anything else. They had less to bring about conflict for. There was no certain positivity in the neutral state they tended toward, but it was almost pleasant—not to say that it was unpleasant. So, I started thinking about other things. Complete understanding was my need.

As I operated our new cash register for the first time, I thought. While I was thinking, I operated the register. After each ringing of a total, there was a bell rung and afterward, the drawer would open. The more the bell would ring the more I would think about the symbolic representation of the bell in our society.

The bell certainly was one symbol that controlled the minds of others. It represented the supposed liberty of the country, and it registered in the greatest strength of self—belief. The only thing greater than the belief was the will. If the will was controlled by the beliefs, the will to accomplish one thing could drown in the belief in another. This must be one reason the world was like it was. How could this have come to be? People are free to do what they want to as long as they do not break the law. The law--that was it. That was how they controlled people—within the limits of the law that could not be everything it was written up to be—not with the situations as they are today. Was it therefore safe to assume that the whole governmental system is as simple as my philosophy? I began with my beliefs, I reinforced my own laws, and I guided my will in the direction of what I believed. Oh yes, they had done the same thing. They (the government of the people) gave misguided concepts of what God's will is and they have people doing and living for the wrong things. From the beginning of American time they have done it. They have the control because they have the belief of the masses focused in just a way to have them doing what they will have them do. Why didn't I see it before? Why was it that others could not see it?

I guessed it was common sense. Along with beliefs there had to be certain fears impressed on people. And fear is the devil himself. Why? Because fear is the basic thing that keeps people from creating and being the beauty that they are.

Why would the government be designed to keep people from becoming what they are? Is it not the most beautiful thought that all people should live in harmony and give of themselves instead of being forced to work, mechanically, just to survive? Why could we not all just share and live happily instead of just living, working and dying? If God created a Heaven on earth, the only reason it has ceased to be is because of its lack of moral reality. How was it that everyone was increasingly religious but patriotism was almost a thing of the past?

And even though we have advanced in technology, intellect and intelligence, we still have the same basic beliefs of old (but not ancient) times. Therefore, we are bound to view the goings on of life and the politics of our country in a unanimous fashion. That makes us unaware of what is actually happening. Yes, there were revolutionists and they were fighting against the wrong things because of a distorted view of reality. All that we did was a manifestation of someone else's dream.

One solution could be to take the Bible and realize the only real message (besides the belief in God) that it attempts to give us, which is to "Do unto others as you would have them do unto you", then apply it daily life. Before that could be accomplished, all people would have to be treated equally. True practice of the message would eliminate the need for the law of the government. The practice of the message could not destroy the government, but the full-swing manifestation of the message could cause the government to destroy itself because of a lack of need for its leadership.

My purpose would be to communicate all such concepts to others, not to preach to them or try to form a group of any kind, for that would take from the individual. The sense of it all was too great to ignore and any group would be unnecessary.

Suddenly I stopped and stood for a moment. All of the thoughts I was having were negative. If there was a positive side, what was it? I would go to one that had some kind of position in the building. He was one of the "top dogs" in the employment department of the building. Therefore it would not be necessary to go to the "top dog" in the law firm, for the employer would know who he hired and why, so he would know what kind of people worked in the building and what they were really there to do, whether they realized it or not. I would find out a positive side of my conception of the "law" in this country.

When I got to his office, I sat in a chair in front of his secretary, Linda's, desk. She was on the phone and she mumbled something, said "okay", then hung up. Then she looked at me and I said, "Is Mr. Hanlin in?"
She said, "No."
I looked back to the side where there was an open door to Rob's office. He looked at me and I said, "Is anything wrong, Michelle? Can I help?"
"There's a conspiracy in this building. You know what I'm talkin' about."

Seemingly puzzled, she said, "I'm afraid I-"

I got up and ran to the mailroom, but Teddy was not there. So I ran back upstairs. As soon as I got back up in the canteen, I saw Stella behind the counter preparing some sandwiches and when she saw me she asked, "What is going on? What's wrong with you?"

I did not answer. I proceeded to service the customers at the register. When I was ringing up the last order, Stacy asked, "Does this have anything to do with Nikki?"

Nikki was a white girl who had sold me some angel dust before. When I thought about it, I felt the supposition was possible, I said, "Yeah, in a way".

In fact I began to question whether the whole mental realm had any validity. When I finished with the customers, I thought some more about what could be going on. I could not find Teddy. Why wouldn't someone tell me what was happening?

Some more people came in. Paula, Sam and Wanda asked me if I was alright and someone else asked me if I was going to the party. When I asked "What party," I did not get a response, so I turned around to ask again and the person was gone.

What party was he talking about? Could this party somehow have something to do with what was going on? No, I was being silly. But just possibly it could. And I knew I should explore all possibilities in 3's. This was the last of three. Was it possible that my thoughts of that morning had somehow been read? Was I just realizing something that they all knew? Was I becoming a part of a realization that they were already aware of?

It was possible that they all knew what was going on my mind all the time, and there was to be a celebration in my honor-- A great welcome. If this were true, then there was room to realize that there were reasons for my failures and accomplishments—a test to see if I could rise from negativity to the ultimate positivity of the truth of the existence of a greater truth and the full realization of the power of the mind. It was the greatest hope I could ever come to understand. I felt that I had the ability to share it with others if it were true. I was overwhelmed with happy vibrations.

I felt a newly-found respect for the people that I had sometimes found intolerable. Could it be that the purpose of life is to lead one to his soul's desire. My desire was to find the truth of existence and the happiness in knowing it. However, I was soon forced to realize that I had just been brought to those who knew a reality that they were going to reveal to me about God. It was a possibility examined and a possibility found to be mistaken.

Then it hit me. Maybe the whole problem with the world was that nobody, not even governments fully realized the possibility of a parallel to this world, which could exist. It was not the system at all, but the spirit of the system which must be redirected. Traditions passed down to us by our fore generations were passed down in ignorant belief of concepts that kept our people in the mentality of the slave, trusting his master before his brother. Brotherly love and human kindness would be the only things to lead to God's Kingdom, and only through brotherly love and human kindness given freely of all spirits, in the hope of pure love, could this kingdom exist.

I believed that human kindness and brotherly love would lead to an understanding of why mankind was created, and bring about a transformation of the mind, spirit and flesh—there would be no more death. That would truly be God's Kingdom.

As it swept my mind that Jesus also spoke of the idea that "The Kingdom of God is at hand", I realized that man's oneness with God's spirituality was the key to the "Pearly Gates". But this spirituality must not be acquired via institutionalized faith, for in spite of its good intent, it also destroyed oneness with God. God created us with likenesses, but He gave us all different minds. Thus, we all think differently and have our own interpretations, which must stem from our own philosophies of what our oneness with God is. Yes I had also remembered the verse that says, "Beware lest you be spoiled by interpretation."

To illustrate to the powerful governments of the world that God's Kingdom is at hand, I realized I must become a living example of that. Since I realized that I had not formulated a way to show God's Kingdom is at hand, I knew that would also be a problem which would take some time to solve. Whatever the solution, it must certainly not be anything that even hinted an air of organized theory, demanding an organized institutional way of seeing things. I knew that there was no such thing as one man having superior knowledge over another, for where was superior knowledge when Jesus himself realized the essence of God? And if we are all sons and daughters of God, we can all realize the Christ consciousness of God.

I did not realize that I had begun to think outside of my pattern in which I usually consulted my philosophy to reason with any situation. I just hoped that that was a sign that the need to reinforce my philosophy with my drills was no longer necessary. If that was the case, I considered it a great accomplishment that I had already begun to live and think within the philosophy I had established for myself. But I had not yet realized that I was also beginning to live without the established philosophies and mores that are the medium of today's society. Because this realization would come so belatedly, it would prove to be the biggest mistake I could possibly make.

Chapter 4
"A Separation of Worlds"

All things continued to make better sense when I thought about them within my new insight, including the reason that certain methods were used and certain conditions continued to exist, when by now, they should be extinct. There was enough wealth to feed and shelter all poor people, and feeding and sheltering the poor would substantially decrease the crime rates. Furthermore, there were ways to help the those who had already committed crimes and had been imprisoned. Society sought only to accommodate, and not to change society's wrongs, and that was society's biggest problem.

The more I thought about the role society played in destroying mankind, the more detestable the idea of authority and government became. Here I was working in a café of a <u>law firm</u> of all places! The idea of a job was no longer significant to me, and I would act accordingly. My priority was to think of a way to change society through government and law; if I was to continue to stay in this detestable law firm, and that would help me change society.

I left my station and sat at one of the tables near the television while I thought. I looked up at the television and the news was on. There was a report on Jim Jones and the Ayatollah Khomeini, both nationally renowned, neither representing anything for the good of humankind. By the sound of the reports, the media was using a whole lot of hogwash organized to dramatically portray roles, for the purpose of simply occupying the public mind. The public would cipher the information then develop more in-depth programs to address the same subjects. It was all crap! It was all used to clone the public. It was all used to leave the average American with a sense of knowledge and perspective, without giving him a direct voice or full understanding in core matters. Was it possible that the governments realized that which they did? It was possible! And everything they taught the masses was nothing but bull crap, and basically only the governments knew that what they taught us was crap. How else could such degrading conditions of life be created without regard to their destruction and humanity? Why else would citizens fight wars? Because of the greed and glory their power-seeking leaders sought. Why else would so few share in the wealth provided by the law firm on the uppermost floors, with a news magazine on the floors directly below the law firm, and the Motion Pictures Association was on the ground floor and lower level. To top it all off, the President, or 1600 Pennsylvania Avenue was across the street.

I did not go over Stacy's that night, I went to Teddy's. He had told me I could go over to his place when I saw him on my way out of the building. He tried to talk to me—to no avail. His questions were on the wrong level: he wanted to know what I had done (physically), and not what I was trying to accomplish (spiritually), so I would not talk to him. I was really hurt that I was not understood. Perhaps, I was only being ignored. Teddy put me in a cab, told the driver the address, and paid the fare. I got some rest when I got to the apartment.

When I woke up, I sat waiting for Teddy to come home and I wondered if there was anything to my philosophy. Was I simply being foolish or was there something to the ideas that ran through my head? Certainly, anything that gave so much strength could not be all wrong, I thought. I decided to stick with my philosophy and be the example I had set out to be. The problem was that if I did not succeed by my example, how on earth would I convince the people that I was right in my judgment of the world? For a moment I thought, "What's the use? I have the cards stacked against me. The most powerful people in the world would directly oppose me". Then I thought "If my experience will leave the world only not quite the same, even if the world does not change, I will have had my effect upon society. So it would be worth it.

When Teddy came home, he asked me if I had any idea what a disturbance I had caused on the job. He said that the people were willing to forgive my disruptions and that I could come back to work, then he told me to get some rest. I insisted that I was not tired and I watched television, noting again how different society was from what it should be.

When I finally lay on the bed, more thoughts ran through my head as to how to approach and relate a transformation of this world to other people. Presently, I was only aware of the possibility of transformation. So in order to effect a transformation, I had to become a part of the spirit of whatever element that would cause the transformation I had in mind. I had to dig deeper and specifically point out the ways in which to transform the mentality of the world.

To help society transform, I had to realize that which was most powerful in society. The most powerful thing in society was the government and I had to realize a point at which the government might be transformed so that social mentality could automatically be transformed.

I began to think. I thought about the beginnings of American mentality in an effort to understand the mentality so that it could be changed. I thought:

"Leaders in our government know exactly the predicaments we are in and they are aware of the brotherhood, love and cooperation amongst ourselves that we have lost, for they created the situations in which those things became lost to us, so that they could create the "royal family" in American society. To create this dream, they must have a people to serve them; a people to build and flourish the nation which they (the government's most powerful people) would rule. So in America's beginnings, people were told about the sense of freedom and wealthy possibilities so that would come and be a part of the great nation. Those peoples were not aware that they would be subjected to being ruled, just like the servant class, which was brought to this country for that sole purpose some years later, if they were unable to make their fortunes in time to stop it. They would have to work and save what they could to make their fortunes. As time passed, these same people received less and less from America, the Great.

Some were at a level of poverty, regardless of their great contributions to this nation, while those who made their fortunes rose to the noble men of each state. And later, when America's wealthy put into writing the rights of the people, she turned around the Word of God (the Bible) to justify two classes of people: those who were wealthy and those who were poor. She concentrated on certain verses in the Bible so that the poor would want not in a land of plenty: she said "It would be easier for a horse to get through the eye of a needle than it will be for a rich man to get into the Kingdom of Heaven."

So after a time came the time when people were individually unable and had become collectively, totally unwilling to work together as the masses of the nation to reverse our situation; the people would not see America for what she really is, for what they foolishly believed her to be (religiously, morally and politically). But if the masses ever did realize America for what she was and awakened to the deliberate, drastic decline of life, humanity, decency, love and freedom, America would fall with its tyrants under the feet of the masses and they would become the voice.

As time progressed, and technical development became America's "new frontier", businesses began to fold and the owners and other people in middleclass positions of America's economy refused to see America for what she was, they were forced to see when everything they had spent their lives building and building upon came under one ownership, jurisdiction, and rule.

The state of all these things existed to date, and I dreaded the thought that it might continue and be accepted. And every artist who demonstrated or expressed human feeling would cease to exist and be forgotten, in the end. People would pray harder to the god of

Mammon that placed them in their state; the god of promise that governed them, the government which had become God to them.

I suddenly realized that the people would have to set an example for the government by combining as much of ourselves together in the interests of humanity, brotherly and sisterly love, and understanding one another, not criticizing our brothers and sisters because anything we have become under the system is greatly due to the system. I hoped that we could become one in society, thereby destroying the lies and institutions that had almost destroyed our will to live within the body and enjoy the ability to touch, hear, speak understand and love. If we were spiritually destroyed we would no longer protest, but mechanically serve the power structure to receive our bread like animals. And that was the disgusting, nauseating paradise that the government sought.

We could reverse it, but would we? Would we forget about competition; would we seek to understand and build foundations of trust and cooperation amongst ourselves, which would eventually sacrifice and eliminate the need for the dollar and leave the power structure upon "The Hill" talking to itself; would we finally become what God wanted us to be: expressive parts of Himself. Would we finally regain the wisdom He originally gave us; would we finally awaken to life as it was before it was influenced by material gain and material wealth; would we do all these things to finally reach realization of life as it was intended to be and begin to gain the skills of building by hand, by instinct and by heart. Would we thereby, reach a stage of life that would place us in such a happy state that, living within it, we would be frequently brought to tears, the spirit of life so strong that it would take life and our minds to places that drugs nor space ships ever would? We should further create, live happily and at peace, giving to the land, not taking from it—we were the only species that destroyed itself for reasons other than mere survival. Would we change so that we could be an example for governments everywhere to emulate? Surely, the only way America would change would be through a change in her people.

Teddy came in and I was still absorbed in thought. The more he disturbed my thoughts, the more I was angered.

The next morning, he told me not to go to the building (where we worked). I defied him because I had a dire need to talk to him. I walked from the apartment down 16th Street about 15 blocks to the job. When I got there, I was told by the security guard that I must leave the building or the police would remove me. I got on the elevator anyway and got off on the 6th floor. There was a kind lawyer on the floor who opened the locked door which led from the elevators to the offices on the floor. When I was unable to locate Teddy, I went into the stairwell and the door closed behind me. It was at that moment that I realized that I was locked in the stairwell because I did not have my passkey. I ran up to the 8th floor. Because I saw a light above me and I knew I was on the top floor of the building, I looked up. There was a window at the top of another flight of stairs, which led to the roof. I waited at the top of the stairs because I knew that the police would be coming soon.

And very soon I did hear the police on the staircase. They searched each floor of the building. I could not be seen from my position, so I waited for the searching to stop.

When all was quiet, I returned to the first floor, the only door to the stairwell which would be open and which was behind a wall, in front of which sat the security guard. When I opened the door on the first floor, police were in the lobby and they heard the door. I was searched by a female officer and told not to return to the building. One of Teddy's friends tried to talk to me. I would not talk to him. He offered to pay for a cab for me, but I again said nothing. Inside the building stood a man I had cursed out weeks before. He proved he was a brother by being there to support me. Yet I could not find Teddy—again. I just walked away in disgust.

About six blocks into my walk back to the apartment, I stopped and sat on a curb. I wondered if maybe I was really crazy. If I was crazy, I still wanted to see a change or transformation, surely someone must feel the same way I did. I began to ask people if they had any change. After asking a few people, I realized that they thought I was begging, so I stopped.

A few more blocks ahead was a circle which was in the center of a busy street. It was grassy and in its center was the statue of a man on a horse. Because a perfect circle with a dot in its center represented infinity, I walked the circle all the way back to my original spot, thinking that if God existed, when I reached the circle's center He would reveal something to me, or I would accept the idea that I had no bounds for my quest for humanity. And God was not real.

When I got to the center of the circle I laid on the grass with my eyes closed. I asked God to show me a sign if what my philosophy had allowed me to see was real and if I was on the right track to want to see a transformation in life. If there was any reality to God I knew that He had to show me a sign. When I opened my eyes clouds raced upward and I pointed my finger for the world to see the formation of the clouds into three perfect circles in a row. For some reason, I covered my eyes with my other hand. When I looked again, the clouds had resumed their regular form.

From that moment on I knew God was real and I would look for His signs.

I returned to the apartment still in a daze, only to find the door locked. I sat on the stairs and asked God to please show me the way to help humanity. I remembered that my menstrual cycle had begun and I was aware of its presence, for I smelled its faint odor.

After Jay returned to the apartment to open the door, he stayed there with me until Teddy returned. I went to the bedroom to lay down. I spotted a little green transistor radio on the floor. I turned it on and I heard music. I remember the song being one by Stevie Wonder. The disc jockey spoke over the song and said my name a couple of times, then he spoke of a party that would be given for me and named a list of stars who would attend the party. So, there would be a party. And Teddy had not told me. I wondered why. I continued to listen to the radio. The disc jockey played more songs. After a while he called my name again. I listened. He said celebrate humanity at my party. Then he played some more music. Sometime while I was listening, I fell asleep.

I awoke to Teddy's voice. He told me I had been foolish and that my Aunt and Uncle would be coming for me because he could not "hack it" anymore. While he continued to "raise hell", I listened and remained silent. He took the radio from me and threw it. He said he did not know what I wanted with a radio that did not work.

I was all too ready to leave when my Aunt and Uncle came to get me. On the way to my Aunt's apartment, she also told me how disgusting my behavior had been, so she also did not understand. Since I had this struggle within myself, I understood how others might look at my actions in a different perspective, but I resented their forcing their opinions on me. They had not understood that I had surrendered my consciousness to my quest. They were beginning to think that I was crazy. Teddy thought I was foolish and my aunt thought I was trying to make her lose her job. Nobody could understand what I was going through except me, and I was too much in my world to explain to people who were so much into the world they had been accustomed to, and not coming into the world I was in. By the time I reached the apartment with my Aunt and uncle, I was disgusted by their unfounded disgust in me. I would protest by not doing anything they asked. I would not even get out of the car, but my aunt dragged me out.

When I got into the apartment, I refused to talk. My aunt called my mother and father. I would not talk to them on the phone, because they had nothing to do with what was going on in my head, not directly. However, hearing their voices on the phone brought me back to thinking about my problems. One of my problems was of somehow finding a way to help my mother who had more problems than she could stand. I knew that if she kept on in the way she had, she would not last long in her body on earth. We were so lost and I felt her every pain of problems, for I identified with them because they were like my own, only more severe. She often said that she felt that with all her struggling she was still going backward a step for every one she gained, or "Hustling backwards." I resented my aunt bringing my mother into my problem when she had problems of her own. I was not, after all, a child. My mother was too far away to be concerned with a distant problem not related to health. And what was she telling my mother to make my mother say that she was on her way to the apartment from out-of-state?

I had to get out of the apartment. I would accomplish nothing as long as I sat there in front of the silly television. There was a typical old picture on television, depicting those dressed in white to be good and those in black to be bad. It was disgusting. I went for the door, but my aunt stopped me. At different intervals, I made the attempt to go out of the door. When I did not succeed, I went to the bedroom. I just lay on the bed wondering if any of what I was going through was worth it. I looked across the room at two formless shapes of lucid light the color of ultraviolet red. I could suddenly feel my grandmother's presence and she had died several years ago. I could also feel my mother's presence. I could sense that they both knew how I felt and that they could somehow feel it too. I was comforted to a degree because of that, but I still had to get out of the apartment. If I could get back into Teddy's apartment, I would at least have time to plan to put my priority of humanity's transformation into effect. I ran for the front door. This time I got out of the door, but my aunt caught me on the stairs. We struggled and she ripped my coat off. I heard a voice ask "Which one of you is that?" I did not answer, but I stopped struggling for a moment. Was it the voice of God? It had to be. Who else knew what was in my mind in order to ask that question? I started struggling again and this time I lost my shirt, but I got outside. I had to find God's voice.

I started running. I ran across the street in my jeans and boots to a parking lot where some cars were parked. I did not even feel the cold of the winter's night. At the parking lot, I got a ride just before police rode over to me. The brothers in the car gave me a shirt. I suppose it was natural for the brothers to approach me sexually in the car when I was running around without a shirt, but the point is that they gave me a shirt and rode me away from the apartment to another section of town about ten blocks away then let me get out of the car when I refused their advances.

All that night, the streets were my abode. The buildings in this section reminded me of the area I had lived in as a child, and I later discovered that the street I walked around was also "U" shaped like my old neighborhood on Barnaby Terrace had been before townhouses replaced my neighborhood. During the night I walked and looked for signs from God. I remember there being something in my mind about the concept of things being polar. I walked around for hours, and I suddenly began feeling chilly. I was seemingly guided to a particular building that looked most like the very building I used to live in. I went to its basement where I heard a generator. There was a brick opening through which the furnace could be viewed as well as the unfinished floor beneath it and a door on the other side, which led into the room. I sat in the brick opening and let my feet dangle.

On the generator, there were some numbers and letters. Maybe all things were signs and being such, I could figure out the signs of the numbers and letters on the furnace. But I could make no particular sense of them.

I began to think about how carefree my childhood was and how, as a child, the free spirit clung to me and guided me to new discoveries. I recalled the feeling because it was now present. Suddenly, I could feel another presence on the other side of the room. I could detect it, but I could not see it. I stood and brushed myself off, then went around to the rear of the building. The door to the room was propped shut by a sick. I moved the stick and there stood a German shepherd. He licked me on my hand as I stood frozen, then he ran away. He belonged to someone because he had a collar and identification tag. I caught hold of my heart and walked around for a while longer. It was now nearly dawn and, for the first time I was beginning to feel sleepy. I went into the hall of another building and saw that the morning papers had been delivered to the apartment doors. It was Sunday because the papers had that usual Sunday bulk. I took the paper from one of the doors and began to read it. I ran across depressing stories on the front page, but saw nothing about celebrating humanity. Finally I put the paper down and sat in a corner to rest my head and arms on my bended knees. Some people across the hall from where I sat lifted me up and took me into their house.

I think I stayed in their house for about two days and during that time, they fed me and gave me a place to sleep. At times I came out of the room where I slept and talked to them, the children, father, and wife. It was obvious once again that what I was saying was not understood by them and they would sometimes laugh. I would be insulted and not want to talk to them anymore. Somehow, however,

I knew that what I was trying to say to them was not complete in its reasoning and, to a degree, I understood their reasons for laughing. I assured them that one day they would understand, for when my reasoning was finally complete, they and the world would know and understand the truth.

The second day in these people's home I was angered by their inability to understand me once again, so I left their house. I had no idea where I was going, but I knew that someday I would repay them for their kindness.

I hid inside of another building. I went down into the basement of the building. There was a green indoor-outdoor rug in a room in the basement, and I sat there on it until I saw the police coming in my direction. I tried to run. I suppose that the way I used my body to express how wrong they would be for arresting me was not effective. I tried to tell them how they should be going after those who were oppressing humanity, for they were the culprits and they were also their employers. What did the police want from me, the physical reality of what was happening in the world or the mental reality of it? By demonstration, I showed them that the physical was nothing, but the mental ability to see through and disregard the physical was the basis for learning true knowledge, which was the only peace of mind. Physical reality was only a piece of the picture. My point was not received and I was taken to the wagon, handcuffed then locked in. They did not understand that they were destroying my ability to express my words of enlightenment, my sun, my light, which they interpreted as being my "son" because they were of the physical.

When we entered the mental hospital, I was taken to a room and placed in a chair and handcuffed to it. There was a television in the room along with several other chairs, a receptionist desk and many other attendants who stared at me. I was turned to face the television. There was a movie on it. It was the movie "Rocky", a rerun. Why could they not see how movies programmed them to think? Could they not see how violence was condoned and how the one who won the battle also lost the war in his mind? There were Black women in the room; as much as they struggled free of violence in their homes, they condoned violence as a sport.

I wanted to be released from the chair. There was a set of 'cuffs on each of my arms, cuffing me to the chair. I kept jolting my arms up to signify my displeasure with being handcuffed. I cursed, demanding that the handcuffs be removed. The more I spoke, the more I was stared at. "They must think I am some kind of crazy animal," I thought. The jolting had tightened the cuffs considerably and I was tired of sitting there being stared at. I wanted to scream from the humiliation of being held captive, wrongly. I decided that it would be best if I was to remain silent, so that the things I said could not be interpreted in the wrong way.

After about an hour (during which, incidentally, I refused to give them any personal information) the cuffs were removed. Before I was shoved around to the elevators, I was again handcuffed, my hands behind my back. When the attendants got me to the third or fourth floor, they shoved me off of the elevator. I would not have been particularly upset if those who shoved me were not of my race. They left me in an area, which had no seats and no escapes. Not long after they left, I began to wonder what was about to happen to me. I did not know why they had brought me to the mental hospital and I did not know if I would ever be able to convince these people that nothing was wrong with me. I knew that I could not speak until I learned how I would get out of the sanitarium.

A fiery red-headed fat lady wearing glasses, a dark guy with an afro and another nurse soon came out of a door that had been locked. They immediately took hold of my arms and I saw a needle that the fat lady was holding. I struggled, and the cuffs grew increasingly tighter. Finally, when the pain was almost unbearable, I ceased to struggle. I was given the shot in my buttocks. I wanted to cry so badly for the pain was so intense in my wrists. I felt as though my hands were slowly being cut off. I no longer had any feelings in my hands. I decided I may as well hold still and wait until all feelings left my arms also.

My jeans were pulled up over my private parts and re-zipped. I was then pushed through the doorway into a ward. The man with the keys to the handcuffs nervously stood behind me. I could feel his hands shake as he worked with the cuffs. It seemed that he had tightened the right cuff. It took every bit of my strength to hold back the tears. I was incredibly angry that I was treated in such a fashion. I had done nothing to anyone. The people who should be arrested are those causing harm. Finally, the man relieved me of my physical pain by completely removing the cuffs.

I was asked a series of questions to which I again made no response. I was then shoved down a hall way and into a room, which was lighted and which contained nothing except a mattress covered with grey plastic and a window with a grill over it. The door slammed shut behind me. I beat on the door until my fists were red. I decided that the employees would not let me out of the room that night. I stopped beating on the door and started looking through a 8"x8" piece of glass in the door, which was my only access to human contact other than my own. I turned my back to the locked door and looked up. I realized then that I was being watched: there was a camera at the ceiling. I looked around the room. The floor was a speckled brown. Looking at the floor closely, I could see the multi-colored specks that make up the light brown color. The walls were made of cinder blocks, painted a light beige. The baseboard was of a black manmade material. The mattress lay in a corner. It was a long time before I finally went to sleep, because I was uneasy as I am when I sleep away from a familiar place.

When I woke up the next morning, the door was still locked but food had been placed in my room along with what looked like cranberry juice. I made up my mind not to eat the food, but I wanted something to drink. I tasted the drink, and it tasted like medicine, so I put it down. I knocked on the door broadcasting the fact that I had to go to the bathroom. Finally some people came and got me and took me to the bathroom, then directed me to another room similar to the one I was in before. Outside of the glass, I could see posters of boats and people. I could hear voices, but I could not see any people.

I wondered what would happen next, and so I was determined to get my complete philosophy together in one unified form in order to conceive of a way that it could be used to get me out of that prison of a hospital.

I tried to unify a concept for eternal life and make eternal life the motive for following one's specified philosophy. It became necessary, therefore, to the cause for death, because whatever caused death had an opposite which would perpetuate and make life eternal.

To me, the life we lived was not fully in accordance with nature, so a full-circle, proven theory for eternal life could not and did not exist within it. It was only the purity of common sense which would point out what was wrong with all of nature (including man) to be able to conceive of what could make it right. When others can be at peace believing what they believe and not tortured by what they believe, I thought they would be able to bring about the forces to bring about peace to all life, and life would evolve into an everlasting platitude. This could not be done unless all men conceived the life of their spirits, for themselves—then would we be able to actually see with our own eyes the wonderment and demonstrations of the miracles of the forces of God. But we could not see the truth through blind acceptance of any theories from any institution. Only through individual conception of life could this transformation come about, because belief, desires and will are the magic forces of our very being. The theories of a few theorists cannot be made the standards for the theories of others, for this was the reason we died and that all other life died: we were all created equally, but we were created as individuals, as evidenced by the fact that we are all different in personality. We do not think exactly in the same ways, do not have the same values, so we cannot be bound by exactly the same ways, and we cannot be bound by exactly identical theories or laws. To do that would be to deny a part of self.

I thought of my mother because she always denied herself happiness and stayed in a state of depression and worry. My father was abusive to us all, especially her. I hoped to someday be able to help her with her problems, but I had so many of my own to conquer before I could ever help her.

Days would pass before I would be out of the locked rooms for good. I was taken to the bathroom at intervals. Some days I would have to urinate on some extra sheets left in whichever room I was to sleep in to keep the urine from being all over the floor. My heart physically ached for a comforting word, a comforting touch, a familiar voice. Day after day I was forced to take a liquid medication for my beverage; day after day, I paced the floor, fighting the sedated urge to sleep and in order that I could protect myself; day after day I refused food; day after day I wondered if I would ever leave that place; day after day I thought and tried to piece the world together, the good and the bad, the positive and the negative; day after day I suffered extremities of cold and hot temperatures.

I wanted to get out of the locked room! I was tired of being treated like a criminal! With all that talk about the power of being, I should be able to leave my body, if necessary, in order to leave the room. I desired with all of the strength I had left to leave the room. Would my will to do so be enough? I thought about it. I brought to mind all that made me want to leave the world and I tried to leave my body by the power of concentration. As I had been accustomed, I laid on the mattress, weak from the sedatives I was forced to take and from a lack of food. I willed my heart to stop beating, and I could feel my heart slowing down. The moment I felt that I was going to sleep, I got up in fear that someone might come into the room while I slept. I began to pace toward the door and when I turned to pace back towards the mattress, I saw my body lying on the floor! I looked down and saw that I was still in a body. At that moment I knew I had a story to tell and I was not finished with life because I was fearful of my new state. The next thing I knew, my body had begun to rise toward the ceiling. I felt as though I wasn't finished and even though something in my spirit spoke that life would hard for me if I stayed on earth, I wanted to stay. I rushed down to my body and laid on it. I awoke to attendants and a doctor taking my blood pressure and pressing my chest.

I opened my eyes and yelled at them to "get the hell out", and at once everyone ran to the door. I did not and still do not know why they ran so hurriedly. Was it because my body was dead or because of the shock of hearing me speak after several days of silence. But I laughed at the sight of four heads looking at me through a crack in the door. That and the fact that I did not believe that I had gone to sleep assured me that my body was dead for a moment.

The following day, I was let out of the room to go to the bathroom. When I exited the stall I had used, I accidentally saw my face in a mirror on the wall. A lot of my hair had fallen out and my face was darker than I had ever seen it. I actually looked as if I had died. When the nurse noticed me looking at myself in the mirror, she steered me away from it and I was taken to a room where the big, red-headed lady and some more attendants waited for me. I attempted to turn away, but the nurse behind me forced me to go forward. The cover-up I wore was taken off of me and I was almost literally forced into the bathtub. It was not that I did not want a bath, which I badly needed, with the stench of menstrual blood on my body; I was not going to be a "show" for anyone and I was perfectly capable of washing myself. I hated the nasty grins on the faces of the people who observed me. The fat lady began to wash me and I just sat there staring at her in anger. Soon she dropped the sponge and gave me the opportunity to wash myself. I picked up the sponge but refused to use it until the nurses and attendants, male and female, left the room. I was instructed as to where to go to find another cover-up, and I found one after I took my bath. I walked around for a while, but I was taken back to another locked room.

The floor of speckled brown was trimmed with a black baseboard that was streaked with lines of dirty water and my mattress, covered with grey plastic, was on the floor in a corner and white sheets lay on the mattress folded. I was shoved into the room and the door was again locked behind me. Why was it that I was forced to stay in these rooms when I had done nothing? I realized that the reason was because I would not operate in any but my own realm of thought. That was why I was here. I had to again become a part of the mentality around me in order to satisfy those who had the power to release me and call me sane.

An agony of the bitter knowledge of having to again submit to any person caused a painful pit in my stomach and a greater pain in my heart. In my mind I knew I would lose a part of the essence of my very own oneness when I was forced to submit just to gain my own physical freedom once again.

I looked out of the little square glass in the door at some of my dear sisters talking outside my door. I looked at them with eyes that had seen the beauty of a dream come true; even though the dream was entirely mental, it was not less. I looked at their eyes and mannerisms. It was as though something within me was painting a picture of their souls. They had learned to accept the wretched conditions inflicted upon the suffering in this country. Though they seemed unaware of it, their faces showed the suffering hollowness of their souls that had totally submitted to a power which destroyed them.

I banged on the door, asking them if they realized how they were destroying themselves. I told them that they looked as if they were dying. I begged them to let me go now, in the night, so that I might remain free in mind. They would not let me out of the room. I cried silent tears. I cried until I was weak with my own emotions and exhausted by my inability to express them or to free myself from the room. I was at the brink of madness.

If I had any doubts before, I was sure now that God truly did exist, for it was only in crying to His name did I calm my mind and soothe my soul. Soon my calm was transformed to anger because I couldn't see why God had not freed the masses of mine and other people in the country who were good and just, who only opposed each other if it was necessary to survive.

Why did God place races of people on earth in suffering and servitude? There must be a reason, therefore I must have a purpose, but what that purpose was, did not seem clear to me anymore. I was not going to be able to live by my philosophy in a world that wanted me to be a servant to man!

I thought about Martin Luther King and I could hear the echo of the Negro Spiritual, "We Shall Overcome" and I sang it to the depth of my lungs and to the top of my voice. I could feel God's presence and it comforted me.

After I willingly accepted my liquid medication (in representation of my cooperation), I sensed the burden of the country's oppression overwhelm me. But while I drank, I asked God to show me my purpose and to let my slumber be one into knowledge of my purpose.

Soon after I awoke the next day, I reflected on the state of the nation in relation to my purpose. I knew that I was given a gift for writing for some reason; I knew that God was going to show me what I should write. I do not know how I knew it, but I knew. My concentration, at that moment, was to cooperate and gain freedom from physical captivity, before I was driven insane by the deafening silence which hummed in my ears, driving me to think thoughts irrelevant and counterproductive to my state of well-being.

An attendant entered the room. When he handed my food to me, I held my head down, so that the words I uttered would not be detected on the camera. I asked him what I had to do to get out of the room and he told me not to try to break out of the room as I had tried to do during the nights. Two more days I remained locked inside the room. I did all I could to restrain my frustration with my isolation. For the second time, the white doctor came in to talk to me, but I knew he was there only to confuse me, so I would not speak to him. I would not speak to him until the day arrived when I spent its night in a room without a locked door. That second day, I was allowed to walk freely around the ward. I discovered that there was a lock on the door that was the exit to the ward. Yet I had made progress for I slept in a room with several other patients that night.

The next day, I was silent unless an attendant or a nurse addressed me. The only exception was one big guy who was also a patient, who was speaking, letting me know he was interested in me. I spoke so that I could let him know that I was not interested in him at different times when he asked. I observed the patients around me. By listening, I learned that some of the patients were ill and that some were not. Those who were "ill" seemed mentally impaired or mentally disturbed by their lives or because of drugs. Others who were not ill seemed to have their own ideas, independent of the ideas forced upon them (although I cannot say that all of their ideas were logical; for that matter, I could not particularly say that all of mine were; I was not perfect). Some seemed controlled by new drugs and I prayed I would be let out of the prison before that happened to me.

I was told that the next day my doctor would come to see me again.

That night it snowed a foot deep, and my doctor was unable to come to the hospital from his suburban home because the new mayor supposedly had not alerted the transportation department maintenance crew to clean the snow from the streets and highways.

I knew my doctor would not come that day. However, I mentally prepared statements for him to answer questions I knew he would ask me.

Another day passed before my doctor came, and during that time, I walked around like a zombie that was too weak to do anything of importance: I could not even concentrate on reading. Yet I was irritable and fidgety. I could not relax. The drug was not helping me, it was hurting me. How could I use that time before my doctor came to take hold of myself if this drug continued to take hold of my senses?

I had finally given the nurse my phone number and received visits from several members of my family and Teddy had visited me. They thought I could look a little better, but knew I was well in mind. My mother and father along with my aunt and a friend of my mother's came together for my first visit. We talked and joked for a while. They assured me that they loved me (and my father emphasized the fact). I asked my mother to leave me some cigarettes. Soon afterward they left. Another aunt came to visit with her special friend and left me a lot of change with which to call her or call home. My older sister came and I was glad to see her and her boyfriend. I did, however, dislike the fact that she concentrated on how bad I looked and told me that it looked as though I was gaining weight. It may not have been her intention, but my very own sister seemed to be trying to bring me down. I realized that was an ugly thought, but it was an ugly thought that she was a nurse and did not practice her bedside manner any better than that. I loved my sister and I was sure she loved me. I just did not know what to think. I made the statement that, if anything, I had lost weight and I let it go at that. It was Teddy who noticed how I held my right hand; I had held it that way because I felt as though there had been a concerted effort to damage my right hand (with the cuffs), which did pain me. I would not attempt to sign any but my own release papers; it would not be before then that it would be revealed that I was left-handed. I did not tell Teddy at that moment, I simply flexed my hand and tried to hold it otherwise as to guide his attention from it.

In the morning, I was called to the front desk of the ward, after medication where my doctor waited. I was glad to see that a sister would also listen to my talk with the doctor. Sure enough, the doctor asked me the questions I prepared. I told him as he asked me question after question that I had ended up in the hospital because I had had an encounter with PCP and that the drug had rendered me temporarily in leave of reason. I told him I used the alias of Paula Green out of my imagination, for no particular reason. I said that I would not speak because the drug, at that time, controlled me and I had the odd notion that speaking was of no service to me. I said I would not eat because I was afraid that drugs would be also slipped into my food and that the last thing I needed was another drug. I said that I had no intention of ever using PCP or any other drug ever again and that I wanted to leave so that I might continue to make a life for myself. I assured the doctor that my actions had been totally due to a drug that I would never use again. I wanted to tell the doctor that I had used PCP a week before I formulated my philosophy and that after I formulated my philosophy I was "in the wilderness" of the city for a week before I reached the hospital and that my actions were those of the soundness of my mind in which I let go of the flawed world around me purposely, in order to gain one of my own to uplift me and to relieve me of a world that was slowly killing me; but I did not tell him. I wanted to tell him that my experience, once it was fully understood by me by the grace of God, would take the form of a book of knowledge for all people, but I did not. I wanted to tell him that his system for evaluating the minds of others was wrong, for it was society which led to madness by making the walls of its oppression crush the minds and souls of my people, but I did not. I wanted to tell him I had not been in leave of my sanity; that what I had was an emotional and spiritual outburst caused by being fed up by seeing people's oppression, but I did not because I had to be free of the prison! But someday, I would tell him. I would not instead be locked up until I agreed that I had been insane and until I allowed him to convince me how I should act, thus lead me from the concerns I had and my instinctive knowledge I had of the needs of my own people, rich in my heritage as a Black woman. I did not tell him that there are movements in thought and that positive thought is stronger because of the productivity of it, but someone having negative thoughts, but thinking they are being positive, can accept the immediately relievable and make it more important than the overall change to the positive. So, if I had had a nervous breakdown, that was what a nervous breakdown was; a nervous breakdown was not a jabbering of what others did not understand, then, in an individual's sudden, shocking and incoherent mentality. It was a state of being in which a person no longer wants to relate to the madness, which is a world reality of 1979; it was, thus, the creation of another world within an individual in order to cope with the mad world around him. It was a realm ventured into when a person so extinguishes concepts from this world of madness that he no longer obeys the mores and norms of but one society—the one within his mind; he is independent in thought and may or may not recognize the ways of the world around him more evidently than his own ways, because of his new mentality. I did not tell him that either.

But I satisfied him. I satisfied him and he agreed that I be released. Before they let me go a brother physically examined me and asked me if I was pregnant. I remembered that I had spoken of a sun (interpreted as "son") on my way to the hospital. I told him "no".

My mother came and picked me up from the hospital the next day. The snow was scraped to the sides of the streets that day. When they gave me a prescription and I had it filled, we left out of the hospital. Freedom felt good! I was absolutely exuberant! I reached the brick walls that sheltered the hospital from the cement sidewalks on the other side of them, walls which had gates that locked me into the prison of the hospital two weeks earlier. I felt deep within my mind that when I walked back into the streets, I would be walking into God's Kingdom.

Everybody's wondering why
When we should all be realizing how
To ever discover and understand
That why is obvious.

Michelle Elaine

Chapter 5
"In the Middle of Things"

During the following year, I continued to build a relationship with Teddy and I finally got a decent job. But I was unequivocally determined that I would not accept any actions from others that interfered with my ability to develop the character and philosophy which would bring me a complete understanding of all things, thus give me peace. And no one did. I believed that it was God who allowed me to seek and not to be deterred by others. When I worked, I made it clear how I felt about all things, when others offended me, tried to degrade me or asked me to do more than my job. The only exception was Teddy. I think I loved him more than I loved myself, at one time, and I would do whatever he asked me to do and more just so that I could say I had a man who loved me as much as I loved him, no matter what the cost.

When I had time to relax, I would meditate. I used to sit on Teddy's bed and look out of the window at the blank sky above the roof of another building. I would stare at the sky, tuning out other sounds around me. I would mentally ask God to be with me and to allow my mind to be absorbed in a telepathic knowledge; that I might be one like the prophets, so that He could do some of His work through me. I would continue to stare into the empty sky and say to myself "I am ready" and just sit there. After just staring for a while, a pinwheel of light such as that of ultraviolet red would spin and spin towards me. I would sit there, tuning out all except the light, concentrating on the light until it vanished or until I was weakened by concentration.

Though I had not felt differently after my meditations I was able to common-sensibly gain understanding of the states of nature around me without the aid of scientific data. (Being a college student, I am just beginning to realize that the common sense deductions I made about nature, as it relates to positive and negative effects on nature, were similar in physical appearance to Darwin's "Survival of the Fittest": To me negativity in all forms of thought and action since the beginning of time on earth, were the causes for the deterioration of life, which was first triggered by Adam and Eve; Darwin notes the adaptation of animals to the environments in which they live and notes that the fittest survive the environment, even its disease. One could say that one of us has a full concept and one of us does not.) All Knowledge must stem from understanding of the nature of the source of life, which is God. The nature of God in physical forms of life is such that negative thoughts and evil acts fester in physical life; the greater the negativity and evil, the more greatly magnified a disturbance is caused in the natural order and direction of nature, and since the order of our universe is circular, the disturbances return to the point of their origination with a negative change—also known as "what goes around, comes around".

All restorative action comes from the conscious need of every living thing's instinct and effort. I knew I would one day see the true restoration of God's Kingdom when His circle was completed.

Late that second year (1980), my mother suffered two strokes and was taken to a hospital in Virginia. I rushed with other relatives to her side.

When we saw her, some of her hair was shaved off of the top of her head. Her hair was grey, brown, red and black, all in one mixture. She looked like she would be okay, but that she would just like to stop struggling and to go on to God. She certainly had the right to want to go on. I had watched her suffer year after year and worry so much that in ten short years she changed from and attractive woman of 35 to a worn woman appearing to be nearly 60 years old. With all her efforts, we were still poor and she did not have anything for herself. She constantly read romance books to keep her sanity and to calm the pressure of the world that caused the high rate of blood pressure that she had, along with my father who had been abusive as long as I could remember.

After several days, I left Virginia and returned home; every weekend for seven weeks I visited my mother at the hospital. It seemed, after a couple of visits, that all the family awaited my return visits. I discovered that the reason was that my mother rarely awoke unless I called her name. I had not awakened my mother, God had. In my mind I had asked God to transfer some of His life sustenance dwelling in me into my mother. Each time I called her, she would awake. It was a miracle of God to me. Yet I knew my mother was so concerned about my reactions to her condition because of our closeness. She was determined to show me she would be alright, so that in itself is probably another reason she regained consciousness. There was no limit to her concern, which led to her state of chronic worry.

After seven weeks and three days, a knock awoke me in my apartment. I put on a cover-up and went to the door. My aunt, uncle and cousin stood there with calm expressions and I said "good morning" then let them in. I knew what they were there to tell me, so I took a seat and asked them what was going on. I forgot who actually said that my mother had died. I even forgot what time it was that she had died. I remembered a prayer I had said to God before I left the hospital where she was being treated for the last time. I asked God not to allow my mother to sustain any more pain than she had sustained. I asked Him not to make her a vegetable after all the love and kindness she brought to the world, making us all children who love deeply from the heart and who would see no harm coming to others if it were in our power to change it. I asked God if he would not heal my mother fully, to please take her unto Him and allow her to be at peace. I asked God to show her the purity of all understanding and wisdom of His Word as she slept so that her mind could be at peace. Most who knew her when she moved back down south looked down on her and she was not able to see her own beauty because of the ugliness of those who shunned her in spite of her loving heart.

I just sat there for a few minutes and said nothing. I remember thinking about how big of a shame it was that a motherless child should rationalize that her mother is better off dead than in this world.

Even at my mother's funeral, many of the people who looked down on my mother all of her life, still looked down on her appearance as it was when she was given her final praise. If it were not for my grief, I would have screamed my anger in seeing their smirks even at the death of one who gave so much to her community. Her appearance had deteriorated. She had stopped being able to get her hair done, her teeth that remained were in decay, as were my father's, she had gained weight. But she was never ugly. And I heard a family member say that one of our cousins commented on the picture of my mother used on the front of the memoir passed to relatives and friends, saying it was at least twenty years old; I could remember clearly when my mother looked exactly like that picture and I was only 21 at the time of her death. Even Mom's own cousins had a tendency to look down on her. It was something I just picked up on over the years, more from some family members than others. I used to think, 'Why don't you help, since you have so much money and so much to say? Or just shut up!' She looked great when you considered the abuse she withstood over the years from my father. He was always violent when he drank too much, and he drank every day.

Coming to terms with my mother's death taught me a lot of things. It taught me the value of giving, for when you give you are fulfilled spiritually if not physically—there is no doubt in my mind that my mother is free and at peace. I learned that in order to sustain oneself, though, one must draw a line be between giving to others and sustaining himself. Trusting one who will not give to you when you need, even though you will give to him when he needs, is foolish. Living life to please any other than oneself and God is placing gods before God and is foolish and unproductive. One must be aware that unless he is in and of the mind to change the world, he cannot reveal the full extent of his love for all people without being trampled upon. I learned to put understanding at the top of my list because understanding is at the nucleus of peace, and full practice of a complete understanding gives righteousness to convictions of brotherhood and breeds the Divine Order of God. I learned to trust God's judgment and recognize that though many things have been accomplished by the prophets, they were accomplished by God's hand and that God could do his work through any of the people on earth He wanted to work through. To be "chosen" by God was to be willing to be an instrument for His work to be done through.

In the months to follow, I continued to meditate; I continued to quiet the outside world, gaze out of the window and concentrate and ask to receive the knowledge of the prophets and observe the pinwheel beams light. Although I did not feel changed and I did not feel more intelligent, I got a certain comfort from my meditations. Still later, though it appeared that I had not learned much from my meditations, I was increasingly able to form my own philosophy of life which coincided with my beliefs about God and, though I was just being made aware of some conditions and concepts, I was able to see an evolution to their individual duties as God's creatures with intent to restore His Kingdom on earth. I knew my duty was to write and give a complete understanding to serve as a foundation for others to complete their understanding, but my own understanding was not yet complete. I was however, able to more readily accept death and I experienced yet another death, that of my uncle. He was the same uncle who had come with my aunt to bring me the news of my mother's death. Uncle Frank died 34 days after my mother died—he died on December 15, 1980, my brother, Douglas' and Teddy's birthday and 10 days before Christmas. Around the time just before my mother's funeral, he had told me that he was having pains in his chest.me and I said he should see a doctor; he said didn't like doctors. But I did not imagine that we could lose him, as well. Mom was 44 when she passed. Uncle Frank was only 35.

BEING

It is a joy to know that we exist
By the source and power, which is God.
We exist in our choice to be with God,
Or to be with and without God,
Or to be as lowly as to be against God,
And we are still graced with being.
We are often confused in life
Or as a consequence of being what we choose to be.
It is joyful to me
That there is such love and grace of God,
To which we have easy access
Anytime we are truly ready
To become a part of the wholesomeness of God,
The blessed pure essence of wisdom.

Michelle Elaine

Chapter 6
"The Second Time Coming Around"

It was early summer in 1981 that I had my second round with my spiritual attainment of oneness. Teddy was visiting his family down in the south and I had invited a friend, Linda, from Maryland to visit with me, who brought her two daughters along with her. I remember feeling an urgency for my book to be finished, but there were still some things that I had not understood. I was yet to know my complete philosophy of life as it related to life after death; nor had I formulated a complete philosophy of why physical life was purposed.

Linda had gone out with a friend of hers and I sat with her youngest daughter, Teresa. Just before Linda left to go for a walk, I had spoken with one of her friends, Andre', who learned a lot from what I had to say about life. I had already come to the conclusion that in order to live life and be in peace, one had to understand life and his place in it, but I could not give him any specifics because my philosophy was incomplete and I didn't have all the answeres yet.

I understood that the truth must be in the world and that the truth must be being spoken somewhere, but how could I decipher the truth in the mass of confusion which was our world. How would one know the truth if it revealed itself before his eyes? Could my previous experience serve as a true of life when it was not complete? What was the missing link that connected my spiritual experience to universal concepts from God, for God truly moved the clouds and showed me many truths. My own church down south left a lot to be desired in understanding. My pastor concentrated on what was right or wrong. In the Bible studies that I did attend, the concentration was to know the characters and events in the Bible, not to understand a conceptual meaning of life and our purpose in life. I admitted that my philosophy obeyed the laws of the Bible's commandments because, of the commandments I had learned, it was natural in my spirit to obey them. I could not blindly accept that after death I would go to Heaven without understanding how it would come to be. Perhaps, some of the teaching of God's Word in my church had not been understood by the elders in my church and they were unable to teach complete understanding. Nevertheless, "With all thy getting, get understanding", and that I would do, for a I would not just blindly accept.

    I was sure that my pastor remembered how long it took me to come to him and accept Jesus as God's Son before I was accepted as a candidate for baptism, when I was only twelve years old. Earlier that week of the church's revival, my mother had asked me if I believed in God, and I told her yes. What else could I tell her? I could not tell my mother who worked so hard that I did not know. My mother had to be driven by some force to go on, and I determined that force must be God. All of the things I was taught about Jesus made me love Him, but I had also learned that we were all the sons and daughters of God and I did not understand why we still had to face a Judgment Day. It seemed that to question in my church was blasphemous. At least that's what I was told when I asked questions. The revival pastor reached me. And I joined the faith. I was baptized believing I could not enter the Kingdom of Heaven unless I was "born again", and that the only way to be born again was to be baptized. Once when I was in church, my pastor said that anyone who ate and drank in communion who did so in vain, "eateth and drinketh damnation". All of that day I was tortured by the fact that I broke and ate the bread and drank the wine with my mind in question. It was not until my problems piled up on me and I questioned if I wanted to go on in the world that it became important to me to completely understand so that I would not leave the earth in question. I feared death because I didn't understand life and wasn't sure about the afterlife.

    I put Teresa to bed and the moment I did so, the pinwheel beams of light began to circle before my eyes for the first time without my concentrating and meditating to summon it. It was golden and similar in color and illumination to the glowing liquid inside a firefly. That in itself brought tears before my eyes. The light never spoke but somehow gave me comfort. I knew that the very next day I should go to the park/zoo where I would receive more insight: It was being in touch with nature which would bring me to true understanding. I could feel my mother's presence along with the indescribable presence of God and something led me to the bedroom. I called out to my mother and Teresa, less than a year old, whom I believed to be asleep, suddenly turned over and uttered no sound, but stared at me smiling. I left the bedroom and went into the living room. Had her turning over been a rolling over and not a seeming pivot only on her right arm the incident would not have seemed strange. It was as though something unseen had lifted her and turned her over with only her hand touching the bed as she was turned. The only time i had experienced seeing something like that was when my brother Adrian fell in slow motion from the top bunk of the bed. There were three of us there. We all saw it. I stayed awake all night in the gladness that I would learn new truths when I was at one with nature the next day.

    Early the next morning, I put on a leotard, shorts and sandals, then walked to the zoo. It was just down the hill from our apartment on Adams Mill Road. I walked in the direction I was guided to walk. I had surrendered myself to the Spirit of God, independent and exclusive of the world around me and the people in it. My concern was with seeing and interpreting signs from God
.

    I ended up by the tigers' pen around some trees and some tens of feet below the point of observation. There were pictures around that showed that the tigers were carnivorous. Then, immediately the thought came to my mind that tigers had not always been carnivorous. I walked over and observed the tigers. When I walked over to the point of observation, they were laying under the trees, but they arose and walked forward. The two of them walked to the middle of the observation point, which was shaped like and arch, then stopped and walked in opposite directions of the highest point of the arch. They walked back to the middle point, then back to their opposite directions again. They repeated the act once more, then returned to their trees. What did that mean?

I continued to walk and I came across a building which was blocked by a wooden fence. I sensed a need to go inside, so I slid under the fence and walked toward the building. Inside there were a lot of glass cages marked for the single domains for certain animals. I, too, knew how it felt to be caged. I walked through the building and arrived at a large room with a large, round, deep space in the center. There was a cement wall of about four feet around the entire space. I walked to the opposite side of the circle. I somehow felt that the two pulleys that extended down into the opening would prove to me, in my doubt, that I was in the midst of an experience where God was truly speaking to me because I would be able to move the second pulley, but not the first. I had been receiving all of my direction from feelings like this. I pulled the first pulley and it would not budge, but when I tried the second, it moved. I began to cry again. Some men who were working the building called to me and asked what I was doing there. Then they noticed that I was crying and asked me what was wrong. I told them that I was alright and left the building. For the rest of the day, I walked around the zoo in my quest for discovery. I was a child in nature, seeking understanding only from God, for I did not know from where else I could receive true understanding.

There was a gentle rain as I walked through the tree-lined paths. I felt so immeasurably at one with nature and I smiled in gladness at the rain that cooled me. I thought about the three M's who had tried to bring peace to the nation. They were Medgar, Martin and Malcolm. What was it that they did not know? There must have been a reason that they did not reach all of the people. What was it? Was it because of their religious beliefs? Should people lead themselves? People might be misled by leading themselves, just as they are by being led by others. Of all of the religions, how could one decipher the one which was correct in practice? Was there one correct in practice? Would it be best for people to live by instinct and intuition in worshipping and acknowledging God? Might that be what it took to be at peace with God? It could be. The rain stopped and the sky cleared. The sun was setting and I walked amongst the animals again. The animals would stop and watch as I walked by. In one instance, I was walking around a circle which was grassy and had an iron-chained fence around it as a barrier. Just inside the barrier, two birds stood side by side, their eyes opened. Neither of them flinched, but one of them had his beak stuck in his back; both of them were of a soft brown and their feathers were trimmed in almost a metallic gold in the calm of the setting sun. I wondered what that meant. My first instinct was not to touch the birds because they were unclean. My curiosity almost got the best of me because I wanted to know if the birds were real, but I did not touch them because of my first instinct not to. And I had learned to do what my first instinct told me to do: I was tired of saying to myself later that "something told me to do, or not to do that". I knew it was God guiding me and whenever He told me to do something and I did not, I always remembered that something that He had told me to do, which always would have helped me. I walked away, and would not touch the birds.

I walked in the zoo thinking for a long time. I wondered why God continued to drive me on in the zoo. I came across a park bench an hour before sunset. I sat for a moment. About ten minutes later I began to walk again.

I walked down the street of the wealthy neighborhood on the other side of the zoo -- white folks' neighborhood. That whole other side of that section of the city, for tens of blocks up was White folks' neighborhood. I knew that the thought had to be symbolic because I already knew that was White folks' neighborhood for years.

I saw a large and beautiful building, which I entered in spite of the questions of the doorman. There was a sitting area to the left with all the beauty of Victorian decoration and furniture, which I loved, but could not afford. I took off my shoes and left my bag and books with them in the sitting room to the left of the entrance. I walked to the third floor of the building. My signs this time would be of numbers three and one. I forgot the number of the door at which I believed the door would open. But I turned the knob and the door opened. I got comfortable. I noticed a lot of pictures which I looked at and I noticed some scrolls with symbols. I did not understand, but somehow I could read from the scrolls something of the succession of my condition and the condition of my people, to this present state; something I cannot recall. I only knew that I was to leave that apartment and I did. On my way to the lobby I had the urge to knock on a certain door at the end of the hallway. I knew that if the person invited me in, he was my friend. If he did not, he was my enemy. I knocked on the door and an old, white man opened the door. He asked me what I wanted and I asked if I could come in. He closed the door. So what if he did not like me or if he was my enemy: What did it mean?

When I reached the lobby, there was a lady at the desk and the doorman stood nearby. They asked me who I had come to see, but I did not respond. They allowed me to get my things from the sitting area, then asked me to leave. I left that building and went to another nearby building. I tried another door inside that building, which also opened. No one was there either. It was not as elaborate as the other apartment, but it was cool and comfortable. I removed my clothes and put on a black slip which was in the room. Then I got in the bed that looked so comfortable. I had just fallen asleep when a tall, white guy appeared in the doorway and ordered me to leave, threatening to call the police. When he left the doorway I got up. But police came with him to the apartment, before I left. My purse and books lay on the floor of the living room of the apartment, but I left them because I could be identified and psychoanalyzed if they were to reach the hands of the police.

I walked away from the building alone. I crossed the street and went back into the zoo wearing nothing but a black slip. In the heat of the day, I was made aware of the lingering presence of my menstrual cycle, which had not quite stopped; it was another sign that this experience was of God just as it was the first time I surrendered myself completely to Him. When I was back in the zoo, I laid down on a bench. I slept in the park that night.

The next morning, I could hear autos in the distance. I got up off the bench and did a sun dance to stretch my muscles. I felt good to awake to the presence of nature. I walked toward another building in the zoo. For some reason I thought of Jesus and opened the door only to see an elephant eating straw. What did that mean?

As I walked around for a while and I came across some buildings that were set up to look like the staff housing at the 4-H camp I had attended one summer. I smiled. It came to mind to observe a particular succession from my neighborhood which a notch or two above the ghetto, to the zoo, the 4-H camp and the wealthy neighborhood. It was symbolic of something, else it would not have been brought to mind, but what was it symbolic of?

I sat on another bench. Soon I heard a truck coming and I stood. The truck stopped and I got in. The older Black man asked me if I knew who he was. He looked like my father, so I said he was my father, my protector. He took me to a building where others observed me in a strange way. I was left in a room alone and I sat there looking around. Soon people came and began to question me, but I could not answer. I would not get in the car when it came, nor would I speak. I was lifted into the car and driven, once again, to the sanitarium.

When we got to the sanitarium, I was taken to a room similar to the one I had been to when I was first there. I was not so closely watched as I was the first time. And I suppose I did not look as deranged; I was out of the ordinary because I was walking around wearing nothing but a slip.

I was handcuffed, but I was allowed to stand. The door I had entered through was still open and it was showering lightly outside. I inched toward the door and when I got close enough to it, I ran, but I was caught.

I looked down to the ground as I walked back to the building, while and attendant held my arm. I was still a child in nature—free-spirited. The ground felt good under my feet.

I was handcuffed to a chair—just one arm this time. I was in front of the television again. I did not react to the program on television, this time of Marilyn Monroe. I sat and patiently waited.

Soon I was asked more questions and again I would not speak. I was clothed and taken to a ward called Nicols 6. When I got off of the elevator, I noticed the scent of Somali Rose (a scent I also wore) heavy in the air of the waiting area for the elevator. I somehow felt that I would not be treated badly this time.

I was allowed to walk around freely for the remainder of the day, during which time I thought and enjoyed the screened-in porch, which had a ping-pong table that some people played on. Then I went to a cushioned chair, which had a back built so that it was at a permanently reclining angle. It seemed a perfect place to meditate and practice my yoga, so that is what I did.

I knew through my experience that a voice would not speak to me, but the appearance of the golden pinwheel light was my assurance that the common sense of pure knowledge was being spoken to my mind as I had asked.

The more I thought the more I realized that the things in America that were of importance to society being nourished physically and spiritually were not being practiced. Only those who suffered the same depravation I did saw a need to protest and demand righteousness. Even my Baptist church at home took in much more money than it placed back into the community, and the community gave the money to the church in the first place. It was as though my own church supported the theory that those who have not, will not have. I believed that I should not say this to the elders of my church in Virginia, for I would be the talk of the town. And what right had I, with all my past misgivings to impose my thoughts on the church? Therefore, I had to continue to form my message, whatever it was, as a universal one.

But why should a land that professes democracy, freedom and righteousness be so opposite to its professions? That I could not understand. Again I wondered if it was all intended that the government should operate this way. Was it not the government's duty to see that righteousness was practiced under the principles that this country was founded upon?

Soon I was stirred from my meditation and full pelvic position. It was dark outside and I was asked to follow the attendants. I did so and one attendant unlocked a door. She stepped aside and I was told to walk ahead. When I was in the doorway, I realized it was another of those locked rooms with a mattress and I tried to push my way back out of the room—to no avail. The door was locked behind me. I decided that perhaps tonight was a test to see my reaction to being in the room. I walked over to the window and looked out for a moment. When I turned around to face the room, I noticed a hole in the wall next to the door—a small square hole that upon observation, tunneled upward behind the wall. I figured out the combination. If I showed no fear and stuck my hand up the chute in the wall, then proceeded to relax and sleep, I would be freed the next morning.

When I awoke the next morning, I looked toward the door. At first glance, it seemed that the door was still locked. I rubbed my eyes and saw that the bolts in the lock propped the door open. I immediately got up and got out of the room.

Most of the people on the ward were gone. I just walked around. It had gotten rather warm in the ward and I saw some people in an office which was glassed in so that patients could be observed. I went into the office.

The office was cool. Someone asked me what I was doing there, but I did not reply. I just sat there and listened to them talk. I looked out of the glass at a sister who stared back at me. I saw the pinwheel light again and it came to mind to look to Jamaica. And I said "Jamaica". The light disappeared. Someone asked me what I had said. I did not reply.

I saw a bookstand in the room which held several blue binders (notebooks) with a succession of names on the covers. I picked up one and it was immediately taken from me. I sat on a revolving stool and began to turn around on it each time I was asked a question. One of the attendants took me by the arm and led me out of the room and sat me at a round table in the area outside of the room. He left and came back out and wrote some things in a blue binder. He seemed remorseful that he should have to do so, and somewhat angered also. He abruptly left the table. It was as though he was saying to me that he did have to report my actions, but he knew I was not crazy and I should stop doing some of the things I was doing. I appreciated that, though I did not say so. He looked at me and rose from the table as abruptly as he had come.

For the rest of that day, I just sat or walked around. I also finally gave the people my name.

The following day, they asked me if I had been in the hospital before under the alias of Paula Green. I said, "Yes".

My Doctor came. Her name was Dr. Plummer and she was a sister.

She asked me if I had been under the influence of drugs. I had to say that I was under the influence of drugs because I could not rationalize my actions to her otherwise. I told her I had been taking "black beauties" (amphetamines) and drinking malt liquor. She made it plain to me that the combination was a severe depressant. She asked me if I was suicidal and I said that I often wondered if it mattered if I lived or died, but, no, I was not suicidal.

During the afternoon of the next day, I walked around trying to piece together answers to the questions posed to me while I was in the park, at one with nature. I sat in the reclining seat and took the pelvic position, trying to meditate. Not long afterward, a tap came on my shoulder, which interrupted my thoughts. I swung out at the person who interrupted, then took hold of myself and took the medication given to me.

At about dusk that evening, I looked out of the screened porch. I wondered what my purpose was. What was my message? I had felt in the zoo that I would be given such an elaborate garden as a home. And of the homes I visited, I knew I would have much better. Why and how did I know that?

I guessed that I should interpret the signs I was given. I walked back to the reclining seat. I observed the pictures of England on the television screen. The basis of America was established in aristocratic England. But that was not the issue. What exactly was the problem in America and could I change it—that was the question.

Just as I was becoming involved in my thoughts, a Caucasian man entered the room. In his appearance, other than his jeans outfit, he closely resembled the idyllic representation of Christ in America. He came into the room with all of his calm and sat across from me. I was immediately angered for I knew the image he was trying to represent.

I spoke to him with my eyes. I used telepathy to project my displeasure with him. He stared at me. I had the feeling that by his staring he wanted me to turn away so I stared at him long and hard until he turned away. In my mind I had battled with him. I remember the argument being that he had also fallen short of the glory and was wrong to suppose that he died for the sins of others. He was no better than I. He had lost sight of the fact that God gave him the power to do the things he did on earth, but he called himself God and that was why he was forsaken: "Thou shalt not have any God before me". The man was apparently only a visitor, for I did not see him anymore after that incident.

That incident made me think in terms of Black and White, wondering why Jesus was represented as a White man when "the people" of his time were all Black. I discovered that I would have to think in terms of how situations in this country got to be as they are today, as opposed to why things are the way they are. That would be the only way to realize the historical design of a system that had become our government, and reveal the reasons for the design. Since truth was not known or was not practiced by our government, according to my understanding and my conception of my philosophy, I had to realize how things came to be as they are and not settle for someone's analogy of why things had to be as they are.

For a while I sat and I realized that what I had come up with in terms of formulating my philosophy was only a lot of realizations. I decided that in order to really gain anything by all my meditating and all my realizations, I would have to think in terms of a beginning to an end. I had to correct what I could of the philosophy I had learned from experiences by meditating and asking for the divine inspiration of truth which God Himself could only give me.

So I began. I asked God to give me a divine inspiration, which of course would be in line with the perfection and balance in nature. I asked God for the knowledge which could be equated with the knowledge of the prophets. I hoped that God would allow this understanding to come about as reasonable, making common sense. I meditated. I concentrated and I began to see the golden pinwheel of light. God, in His infinite wisdom, understood that thinking common sensibly was the only way I could accept His Word, for no mere voices or pictures could possibly represent Him to me, for to me God had no form and I would only look at the intangibles, such as the light to represent his presence—a light I summoned, which no one realized I saw.

Understanding that the Bible could not have been the beginning, for God's existence was before the Bible, I had to look at God as the beginning. Since there was no way to define God, I had to think of Him as the source from which all things came into existence. God was the source. But knowing that He was the Father and Mother of all things, I knew we were His children, gifted with reason and understanding given to us by God. So we were components of God even before birth. That was the "we" and the "us" spoken about in the Bible when God said "Let us make a man". Man became a living soul. He (man) walked the earth and was given woman with whom he could find companionship. The two of them ate from the only fester in their garden of paradise, the desire to know and understand His paradise; this understanding was impossible to attain except in the oneness of the spirit of God, which neither man nor woman could acquire completely except in pure spirit, for the physical form was imperfect and limited in itself.

Being of God and knowing that God had a plan for man was man's reason for being in the garden. And God had told man not to eat of the forbidden, for how could He perfect him? But this may have been God's plan—to give man an independent mind to test his trust. And if man would live independently of the father, he should be left alone to realize his mistake and to, of his own will, become of mind to return to the Spirit of God, not wanting to be independent of God, for God was the only source to which he could return to purify himself and have truth. Therefore man should return to God on his own and be independent of those whom might lead him in the wrong way, claiming to know the truth. However, man's being independent was not all bad: If man should come of the mind to know and realize the nature of God, in death man might become companion for God. It was probably Lucifer's (Satan's) mistake of wanting to be equal to God which caused his fall; nothing could possibly be equal to the source. Defying the source caused the first of falling and defying Him once again would cause death (physical). Therefore, God had to allow birth until such time as man would return to the source on his own accord, for to make man as angels might create another Lucifer. During the passing of many suns, man did more and more which was unpleasing to the nature of God, and man became less and less like God. Man's walking in the garden caused the garden to be less and less like God's creation of it. Physical manifestations came about in the death of nature and the festering of wildlife which caused an eventual counteractive effect upon all life, in which all life that previously perpetuated itself now devoured itself. And so in the midst of the land did garden pests fester a new kind of life and did carnivorous natures develop in animals and man. As man became less and less in tune with God, he knew less and less when he was born over generations.

The extent to which a man rebelled against God was the extent of his rebirth into forgetting—man could not die completely because he was given a spirit. It became evident that trust in the spirit of God was the only way in which man could ever know the nature of God and understand the purpose for our existence. It is only in the practice of a trusting belief that what is practiced is the will of God, that man will counteract the festering of life and see that day that sickness, death, carnivorousness will cease to exist and man will once again become a living soul, not the dying one he was. The disappointment God beheld when He was first disobeyed could only be corrected by an honest effort toward this directional goal. The effort, the pressing to live according to God's will, and the manifestation of it, in this our lives, was our beginning to end, regardless of the in-between. I was going to be in recognition of the beginning, realizing that my defiance was the reason I was now to the point of wanting to fight to help man live closer to God's law of the beginning and ending.

The light disappeared and I sat wondering where all of these thoughts came from that made complete sense to me.

I felt better for the rest of that day. My doctor had told my people to bring me something to wear. The next day, I would leave. I felt good.

The next day came and I sat around. I took my medication when it was handed to me. I ate and generally cooperated throughout the day. I was told I had to go to the doctor that day. They took me to the doctor (dentist) who looked in my mouth, then let me go. When I got back upstairs, I gathered my things and before I left, we had another of the rap sessions with all of the patients. Soon afterward, an attendant gave me a pair of flat, round, gold earrings which had the pinwheel shape molded into them. She said, "Remember Nicols 6" and I said "I will". Then I left.

Chapter 7
"A Complete Philosophy"

It is 1984 and I am just finishing my book. There was a lapse of time that passed (3 years) during which all of the missing concepts in my philosophy came together.

There had been a reality to what I had gone through and to all of the understanding that I gained through "my experience". I did not, however, have an organically whole philosophy. There was one specific reason that my philosophy had not come together: I did not know for sure that the things revealed to me were real. There was no group, no individual that seemed to have the same ideals of my philosophy that I had, and I questioned whether or not the things that I saw or the understanding that I had received, was either real or sound. If the truth as I understood it had no actual basis in fact, I could truly be considered as being insane. I felt I could have been unable to receive the reality of truth because of a possible misguided perception. Additionally, I still had a few questions that were unanswered.

It was on the eve of Easter Sunday, 1984 that I read a small booklet. Teddy and I had gone our separate ways many months earlier and I had become involved with my love, comfort and physical protector, Rashad Muhammed Rasuala. We "fell in love" having a mutual outlook on life and a mutual direction in life: to spread the Word of God as purely as possible and to share The Word with those who were young and misguided. In an effort to understand the man I would someday marry, I read some of his books and I had begun to read his Holy Qur'an.

I immediately noticed the difference in the presentation of the Word in the Holy Qur'an, as opposed to its presentation in the Holy Bible. There were different prophets spoken of than in the Bible. That led me to believe that perhaps Islam was recognizing different prophets for religious reasons. When I discussed this with Rashad, I learned that Muslims did believe in God and that they did also believe in Jesus and Moses. There were many other prophets not included in our Holy Bible that are included in the Holy Qur'an. Finally, I learned that Al-Islam means "The Truth". And that budded full curiosity in me to seek what truth I could learn from Islam. I was hindered insomuch as Rashad and I were students and had our responsibilities to our education. However, I went home with Rashad to visit with his family over the Easter vacation. I knew that his parents were Christian and that they did not approve of his becoming a Muslim, so my learning would be quiet and would be acquired through my reading.

On the eve of Easter, Rashad had visited a friend, Nadeem, who had given him a booklet to read. Because the booklet was entitled "Warning to the Government of America", it immediately struck my attention. The booklet was of a speech given by Minister Louis Farrakhan (leader of the Nation of Islam) in Washington, DC on August 15, 1981.

Perhaps it was because I was seeking the Truth for several years that when I read the booklet I was able to see. But it had been a saying in my father's house the "the truth outshines the lie" and that was the true basis upon which the booklet helped me to see the truth.

The subject of Minister Farrakhan's speech was "The Time and What Must Be Done". Minister Farrakhan spoke of the fact that we have not and probably would not receive justice from America, a country that would not in its present state support the well-being of all of its citizens. And I admired Minister Farrakhan's ability to deliver his address and to show the undisputed truth in the process.

I realized, first of all that the Minister had nothing to hide in Islam, for he used our book, the Holy Bible, to illustrate his points: "The book of Genesis tells us that the people of God (Abraham's seed) would go into bondage for 400 years. Abraham was tried by God. God saw in Abraham much value. God told Abraham that 'your seed is going to be a stranger in a land that is not theirs, and they shall serve them and they shall afflict them 400 years, but after that time I will come and I will judge that nation (very specific pronoun, that nation) which they shall serve. And afterwards, shall they come out with great substance.' The signs of that nation is given as the children or Israel. But I heard Mr. Cronkite questing Mr. Sadat one day at the base of the Pyramids in Egypt. Mr. Cronkite said to Mr. Sadat, "It is something that we are here at the base of the Pyramids, built by Mr. Begin's people when they were in bondage here in Egypt". Mr. Sadat looked at Mr. Cronkite and said, 'We have no record of that in our history.'"

That is proof that we are lied to every year, for we are taught that Israelites built the pyramids.

Minister Farrakhan continues, "I say to those who call themselves Jews, who have gone out to steal the history that is written in the Bible of the people of God to make themselves what they are not, if that Scripture is not referring to you, and it is not, then what people is there in the annals of history who fulfill the prophetic picture given in the Bible and the Qur'an as the people going into bondage? Moses is the key man of the Old Testament and he is one of the most oft-mentioned prophets of the Holy Qur'an. Why? Because Moses is most significant to the events of our time today.

"How long have you been here Black man and woman? Let us see. Go to the Congressional Library in Washington since you are here, and check out when they say the first black man was brought to these shores. You will find that it says that first black man was brought here not in 1619, but in 1555, on a ship named "Jesus" piloted by one Sir John Hawkins, or Sir John Hopkins. From 1619, if you subtract 1555 you get 64. Sixty-four represents the hidden years that transformed you from a wise African to a foolish slave in America. Some of the wise historians said that America, knowing Islam, knowing the power of the ancient Muslims with whom they fought in Europe, did not want any Muslims in America, even though many of the slaves that were brought were Muslims. You could hear them on the plantation, "Allahu Akbar, Allahu Akbar.' God is the greatest. "Allahu Akbar, Allahu Akbar.' God is the greatest. The white man didn't want any blacks in America who knew that God was the greatest because when you know that God is the greatest you can fear no man."

There are some 2000 tricks used on the Blacks in America today to keep them ignorant. But the time has come. To date, 429 years have passed since we have been in this country."

Minister Farakhan continues and says that the end of the world is coming to the American government and asks some very pertinent questions of the American government and all of those who are dictators of it or practice it:

"How come the weather has changed on you? How come the elements, the sun, moon and stars, are not with you anymore? How come the flies are against you now? How come the boll weevils are against you now? How come the fire ants are against you now? How come the wind and rain have turned to be your enemies? How come the sun that used to be your friend is drying up your plains now? How come the tornadoes, the twisters, the storm clouds, the plagues of disease are on you now? How come the nations of the earth are turning against you now? I'll tell you why, sir, with all due respect: It is because God Himself is angry with America; angry because of the evil injustice done to an innocent people who have never done anything of harm against America."

Minister Farrakhan made plotting against Blacks in America still more evident:

"We (Muslims) pooled our resources, knowing that your school system has destroyed our minds. We built 46 independent little schools around the country. But the government of America was working diligently inside and out to destroy schools that taught babies discipline. What is it that you fear, America? You fear the knowledge that Elijah Muhammad was revealing when he said that Allah revealed to him your nature; that your nature was evil; that you are by nature, the devil. Well, if Muhammad and his God are liars, then why don't you go before the world and prove that you are not the devil by doing righteousness?

"The President said, 'We need dialogue; we need to get to know one another." That is what God came to give, the knowledge of ourselves and the knowledge of others than our own self. We know you and you know us. There's no need for us to talk to get acquainted. We have had 400 years under you, watching you night and day, watching your history, seeing your footsteps in the sands of time. We know you. And you know us.

"Poor Elijah Muhammad, the government jailed him when America went to war. Not because he was a draft dodger, he was too old for the draft. But they didn't want him on the scene teaching you peace while America was prosecuting war because America needed young black bodies to help her win the war. Put the man in prison. Elijah Muhammad took our nickels, dimes and dollars and set up business. You said in your speech, Mr. President, you need more minority business. Elijah Muhammad was giving black people jobs. Why did your government work to destroy his work? You sought to destroy his work. You put paid informers among us to try and destabilize our work; to corrupt our work. You put reporters to feed stories into the news and television media to make us look like convicts and thugs and criminals so that when you and your police department came down on us, the people would thank you for getting rid of us.

"You plotted against Elijah Muhammad's life. You, along with the Arabs, worked to destroy the Nation of Islam. This I know. You used hypocrites of Elijah Muhammad's followers—even out of his own family—like they did Judas, you did the same. Now, you say you want to be our friend. How can we trust our friendship? On

82

what basis would we be justified in trusting your friendship? I must respectfully say, Mr. President, we are going to rebuild the Nation of Islam. But how will you respond?

"Will you train black FBI agents again to come among us? Please don't do that. Please don't do that? Please don't do that. We are not gangsters. We are not drunkards. We are not thieves. We have given all of that up. We're trying to live righteously. So, if you send your agents among us to try to disrupt our peaceful and righteous work, please, sir, we will have to answer that this time. Any black man or woman who would dare work for the United States government as an agent of theirs to destroy the work of righteous men and women, I tell you from the depth of my heart, we will chop off your head and personally deliver your head to the head of the FBI. We will make sure that all other agents who have that sick idea in mind, when they see your head delivered to the heads of the FBI and the CIA, they will remember, 'We better not go there making mischief among those people.'

"We are determined to be free"

It was not until further in the booklet that I realized the full extent of the white man's evils against my people:

"In 1932, the United States government, along with the Joint Center for Disease Control in Atlanta and certain states, entered into a conspiracy. 400 black men in Alabama were either infected with or were found to have syphilis in the last stages. And when syphilis is in its last stage it affects the cardiovascular muscles, or the heart, and it affects the nervous system and deteriorates the brain. 400 black people. They would not treat these men. The government was behind it. They allowed them to multiply, have sex, travel, and spread syphilis. 40years it went on until 1972 when a suit was brought against the government and the other parties involved. It was settled out of court: $10 million. You figure 400 men with syphilis on the last stage, nobody treating them; it was against the rules to treat them. They were told that they had bad blood. They were allowed to multiply, have sex, spread syphilis. How far has it gone? Is $10,000,000 compensation enough for such wholesale wickedness?

"Dick Gregory said that in 1962 they called all the children to be vaccinated against polio. Mothers took their babies to be vaccinated thinking that they were getting a polio shot. Later they learned that what the babies were given was a polio contaminant called SV40, which is cancer itself. Twenty-five years ago, cancer was a white man's disease. Twenty-five years later black people lead in cancer. How did it happen? The cancer research center in Washington and the White House admitted to Dick Gregory that it was a tragic mistake. The government was behind the syphilis experiment. They were behind the polio program. The government of America dropped germs in the air to test the population of San Francisco, and went into the subways in New York with a light bulb filled with germs and dropped it in the subway to clock how far the germs would go. The government practiced putting LSD and other mind-controlling drugs on black soldiers and blacks in the penal institutions, blacks in the insane asylums; all government sponsored. In Washington, D.C., there is a tremendous influx of high potency drugs. Blacks are dying like flies: O-D'ing. Meanwhile, white people want to take back Washington; too many black people in Washington. They moved you out of Capitol Hill, they want to move you out from where you are now. What means and methods are they using?"

I realized that the voices of Muslims which I had heard in the past were not screaming of an old grudge because of the slavery that our foremothers and forefathers suffered in the country, but because of the "undercover" reality that we were still being enslaved and if we would not be slaves, we would be slowly, but systematically killed. The government in America was seen for the devil it really is. And for 429 years, my people have suffered in this country and all the games America plays, telling us that in years of economic struggle that she will finally find us jobs was also a lie to keep us under until still more tricks could be played on the Black people, so that by the time America delivered jobs, blacks would have destroyed themselves even more and have destroyed their ability to act with drugs, allowing Americans to develop more tricks to keep us down."

All of that shed a new light on the subject. None of what was being revealed to me as it related to injustice and conspiracy against my people was incorrect. And America was not alone, for the Jews, be it or not to their knowledge (as a whole), assisted America by keeping some of God's Word from us. Anyone in America who was Black would be foolish to still believe that the White man in America's government was his friend. There were some good people who were White, but the existence of the Klu Klux Klan in full swing was evidence that the old white man is not our friend, for why would he instead insist that we destroy the Nation of Islam? And why is it that every president in America up until 1984 is a member of a White masonry and in the upper third of the organization's membership? What is the White masonry that all of its leaders destroy Black people?

There was one thing for sure, there was still a concerted effort to destroy Black people in America. Black people in America were some of the people of Abraham and the chosen people of God who were to go through bondage in America for a duration of 400 years before God would return and free them completely from their enslavement. God chose to test the seed (or generations) of Abraham, then He would judge them and He would also judge the seed of their masters.

Perhaps God wanted to see if the seed of the slave masters would be as worthy as the seed of Abraham. If that were true, sorely would the seed of the slave masters be judged. But just as all of Abraham's seed are not good, so is it true that all of the slave master's seed is not bad. There would be the chosen of all races that would receive God's grace when He judged humankind. Surely, the knowledge of how to completely achieve life eternal would not be revealed until the judgment had come. And I knew that there was at least one among us who desired eternal life and thus was living the reality of beliefs in God, life and self, which I felt would be pleasing in God's sight.

The fact still existed that I, as one of the seed of Abraham, was chosen from the start. And I had endured in my lifetime. But knowing that without unquestionable belief in God and the understanding of the purpose of God's earth, and being unable to place myself in the events of the coming of God's order, I was sure that a change in me and others would have to happen. Surely, if the circle of life was to be completed, life would turn around and again become eternal in His people But only would the worthy receive eternal life.

To be worthy would mean to be conscious of change as it came and to be conscious of how one should act to come into being one of God's people. In my philosophy, I had already realized that man must live in complete harmony with all others who aspired to act as agents for God. We would have to learn to harness our physical wants for an eternal need to be at peace and be receptive to true understanding. It was only the full knowledge of what would be eternal that would show us what was not eternal. Spirit was eternal, the physical was temporary. The desire for the eternal should bring about a lack of need for the temporary.

But the true test of Abraham's seed was to be in a land in which only the physical mattered and to make the seed of Abraham realize that the physical was a nothingness compared to the eternal. For it was Adam's and Eve's inability to see that the physical was less than God, who created it all, that caused their fall from the grace of God. Once this principle was understood by those who would be given eternal life, defying God for the physical desire to eat, smell, touch, taste or hear anything rather than God, would start the circle (cycle) in the individual again. We had to understand as God's creations so that we would know how to remain alive as his creations, but we had to realize that God will not create others just like Himself, for to create another just like Himself would be to recreate another source. He is the source. Surely, if God had given Lucifer (Satan)), a former angel all of His attributes, the physical would be all that mattered in life, and the seed of the slave masters would be God in this country, and so would Satan.

God, the source of life from whom all wisdom originated and from whom all knowledge shall be given, is the only one who holds the gift of life, He is the wise and powerful who saw the need to test the seed of man in order to decide whether man is worthy to live on and on. But God in his wisdom recognized that Abraham's seed was being destroyed by an ignorance of its place or purpose in America or in life. Therefore, his seed could not be judged fairly unless the nation would fall in its current spirituality, and then a nation of

God's Word would rise and awaken Abraham's seed to its purpose in America. Then Abraham's seed would be able to see the light of the right path and again have the choice of the spiritual over the physical. It was wise not to show us that it was our purpose to go through these 400 years for a long time, because we would have willingly accepted the punishment for years and would not have learned and would not have a reason for a buil-in spiritual hope and humbleness.

Surely this was always destined of all humankind so that only the worthy would live in the spiritual presence of God and accept it with gladness, knowing Him for more than His existence and the feeling of His presence, but also for His essence, understanding Him, loving Him and being nourished by His power because we know Him.

I will rise to the higher plane and evolve with the spirit of man, for I now know the equation: to live in the knowledge of the test and to be philosophically the same as I believe God expects of me, and be what will lead to my spiritual evolution and revitalization, rebirth, and restoration into oneness in spirit with God.

Chapter 8 –
My Philosophy—The Evermore

I am a creation of God and I have been given the imperfection of choosing in my spirit to live in harmony or disharmony. Subordinate as I am, I cannot have the ultimate wisdom and perfection of God. But I submit that I am what I believe is vital to peace. I am best as I can be in oneness with myself and the part of God that is me.

I do my best to live to the full beauty of goodness and humanity and brotherhood which vitalizes my spirit and is my joy in life.

What is real is the spirit of good and the spirit of happiness, which gives life the very strength to thrive and makes life wholesome and peaceful and carefree. I live in the truest form of love in spirit as I can, restricting my pleasures in life only because they cross the line into what is wrong as to my understanding of what wrong is as it relates to right in the sight of God. For love we bring to life and pleasure we bring to the body as long as it is not wrong in the mind and spirit, which beholds what is wrong in the eyes of God. This cannot be dictated to me in principle, because it is my evolution within my mind and until my understanding evolves, my soul cannot. I cannot separate God's purpose from my life and my love and my pleasures, for to do so is death. I should instinctively know what is destructive to my understanding of God, His purpose and our reality in oneness with Him. If we could evolve we could become companions for God by his direction and wisdom guiding us. And we cannot see how to evolve if we do not remember and keep in line with evolution of spirit. We cannot become like God unless we are like God. We will deteriorate and die if we do not change. It took 400 years for one of a seed to learn this and give it to others in pure oneness with the giving of God. Unless we are willing to learn, we destroy His every effort to create others like Him with wisdom. It is an evolutionary process of spirit and wisdom. Unless we become in spirit like God, we destroy His purpose to help us create Him in us, evolving us to being like Him, knowing that it could vanish in the blinking of an eye, should we as spirits debase ourselves and return to a lower plateau in which we must struggle again by repeating phases in evolution, learning and returning unless or until God feels a uselessness in His spiritual exertion with the spirit. I can only ask and hope for the evolution of my spirit through practicing what I believe to be right and thrive in likeness of patience and love, and believe that the oneness will be revealed to me until I become like God.

I should be able to feel the spirit of God in me, guiding me, telling me what is right so that I may participate in my evolution and be sure that the evolution is taking place. I know that the evolution means finding answers to all questions I have, which God shall illustrate in answer for me by way of His signs. But I shall not forget the world around me, but write and write again until I can see that my evolution is progressing by making sure that my understanding is as complete as I can, before the next phase of learning shall come. All learning will be by the guidance of God.

My motivation in life is to attain oneness in spirit because of my understanding, and to be as much like God in my mind and actions as I possibly can.

I should write during spans of time that I feel that something has been revealed to me by God so that I do record each phase of learning and understand it step by step. Then I should live by what I learn if it is in line with understanding and progression of my spirituality.

When a greater understanding should make me realize that evolution will better take form in a change of my way of thinking, I should change my thinking for the betterment of my spirit. Unless the change will be better, it will not be shown to me by the logical demonstration of God's signs, which will be shown me by God's explanation that there is a greater basis of spirit as expressed in the first law of my philosophy—evermore.

The expression of my Philosophy-Evermore is a way of expressing what I believe is God's individual creation of my spirit. My expression of my spirit is the basis upon which God can determine, and decide how He should thus help me to evolve. My evolution is to be only different in the fact that I am different or that I am individual. The way that I come to see the evolution will be different, but the final outcome will be the same as many; an outcome of oneness with God, not being God, but being like God, unable to be like God until or unless I am like God. Not able to be like God if I am acting, thinking or being unlike God.

I can only be bound by what I consider to be knowledge or truth and true to practice in the knowledge of that truth.

What I am bound by is not and cannot be what others are bound by, for we are all different and our lessons taught by God for the purpose of evolution will be different, and may also be misinterpreted by others whose learning comes in a form or forms to best suit that individual.

Those who would tell others what to believe do attempt to take God's place in the evolution of a person's understanding, involving the increase of his spirit. Those who attempt to take God's place blaspheme God for God will bring forth knowledge of what should be done and no one else has that power. People who take God's place destroy His efforts to bring knowledge forth in our spirits and they cause confusion and misdirection. I should, however, listen to the knowledge of others, for others might bring me the words and understanding of God. I will know when the knowledge is knowledge God wants me to live by, for He will illustrate that through other signs.

Knowledge is not how many words I know or how many specimen I can analyze, but in the recognition of one thing that flourishes as opposed to another thing that deteriorates life. It would be best to follow what best flourishes life (God) to evolve into greatness of being. To look to that which deteriorates life will be evidenced in my spirit's deterioration, (but only after God should make me physically without worry, thus without troubles of finance will I be able to look only to that which flourishes life and my spirit.)

God will make all necessary changes in life to suit the ability for the evolutionary changes in my spirit.

All pieces that relate to my coming of oneness in my spirit will remain a part of my spirit as I learn through God's signs to be more like Him in spirit.

I will not be tempted to act outside of what I believe God wants me to do, nor do anything I feel He will disapprove of. I will accept no other ideas than those I feel God wants me to live by.

The best way for me to find and experience oneness with God is to disregard all that others tell me "is", other than the happenings of the events of history, up to my point in the circle of life, which better helps to illustrate the existence and direction of God's plan. Never should I shun another for his understanding, but share my own in a mutual respect and desire for companionship and understanding.

Anyone alive has the same chance to evolve in spirit, but they cannot evolve with any evil whatsoever. Deterioration is not a matter of physical evil, but of physical wrong as it relates to spiritual development and evolution. The wrath and anger of God only comes when one cannot realize a spiritual realm because of a physical reality.

Before physical realities overtook our spirits with the need to have the material in order for us to survive and evolve, the progression of evolution of spirit took place more rapidly as with the prophets. It is necessary for God to intervene so that we can all progress and evolve in spirit, if it be our choice to do so.

I can never determine that others' beliefs are wrong. I can only live by what I think is right.

I should share my understanding with others, but all the understanding I share, I should know why I believe it to be understanding, for that is the only way I can be justified in expressing my understanding as knowledge, which is only knowledge to me because of my experiences with the illustrations and revelations of God. Whatever I determine is a real is based, forevermore, on the things I believe to be in line with the truth (as I see it), that all of life is for the purpose of becoming companion to God. Something of spirit is what we are, something God can someday mutually communicate and relate with, something that He created. Life is eternal and the living of the spirit of creation will be the aftermath and legacy of being true to the spirit of God.

Because my understanding has led me to believe that the Nation of Islam is the closest group of people who have in mind the same principles of brotherhood and harmony, it is now my way of life with others. Surely, I was a Muslim before I, of Abraham's seed, was scattered in a strange land. I have returned to my state as a Muslim and I submit to what I believe in my learning and understanding to be the Will of God. I have the knowledge that I believe either can be equated with the knowledge of the prophets, or that which has given me such understanding and peace of direction and purpose of life. The elements in material forms of life serve to illustrate the stages taking place, metaphorically, in the mind or spirit, for better or for worse.

I submit that I have an understanding of how many things came to be, thus I understand why many conditions are present, so I have an understanding of how to effect change, and I recognize the signs of God to see change or evolution as opposed to "de-evolution" or deterioration. I will understand the previous work of God through people on earth from cover to cover in the Holy Qur'an, for in practice, Islam is the closest religion in practice to God's Divine Order in America and the world over.

I believe that the purpose of a Muslim attribute is to emphasize a person's gift and purpose in life. My attribute is Adeeba Aqueela Rasula. Adeeba means writer, authoress. Aqueela means gifted with reason and wise. Rasula means messenger.

It is with great feeling that I sense that this is not the end of my spiritual evolution during this physical life. I only hope that you, the general public are able to read this and that I am able to more rapidly evolve because of a lack of worry with the physical reality of finances. I am in the privacy of my own home, surrounded by the quiet and peaceful spirit of nature. I do take time to recognize fully (at less lengthy glances) the revelations of God for what they are.

My children will be yet three other chapters in my life, and I do not believe I am pregnant, but I know. Often, it is true that it will happen when I write something before I understand it. That is so strange but true......

.....With this, in 1984, I thought I had "arrived" at my spiritual destination. Nothing could have been farther from the truth.

INSIDES OUT, PART 11, The Middle-DIMNESS (The next 25 years)

Chapter 9

And at the end of my spiritual journey, I believed I had arrived at the truth because I had found Islam. Islam was my first and true understanding, because Muslims also educated me about my condition, our condition as a people in America, and because the information I received from them was factual, I believed Islam to be "the Truth". I studied Islam and I read the Qur'an. I worried that few in my family had come to know "the Truth" and I would need to bring the truth to them and others by publishing my book. I doubted that I could ever change what they believed and save them from themselves because I believed they were brainwashed and that it may take an act of God to force them to face the truth. They believed in a white Jesus whom the White Man gave them to worship, to follow. Didn't they know that the whole New Testament was a lie? Who could possibly believe that God "begat" Jesus? If anything was blasphemous, that was. Jesus was merely a prophet. There was no "Son of God" in the sense that they believed Jesus to be. We were all sons and daughters of God, and none of us was above the other. Throughout the history of the Bible, God sent prophets, and Jesus was one of them. The final revelation was revealed to the Prophet Muhammad and through that revelation the religion of Islam was born, a way of life. Islam was my way of life.

I completed my course of study at St. Paul's College. I had to return to the College in June to graduate, because I had completed my courses by December. During that time, I had become pregnant (around April 1986) by my fiancé, Rashad. When I graduated in June, my pregnancy was barely visible. Not so when we got married in November, and the baby was due in January. I got a job at Jefferson Savings and Loan and Rashad eventually got a job as a corrections officer for Buckingham County's Department of Corrections (DOC). I continued to study Islam and the practice of its traditions, though I did not wear traditional Islamic attire. The most basic practice I performed was the ritual of prayer, five times daily.

Rashad and I got our first apartment which was an efficiency (studio) apartment just outside of the Buckingham Courthouse area in Buckingham, VA. We had first been staying with my brother, Eric, then my cousin Bruce. But we got our own apartment because of the baby. When our baby, Sheba Rashida was born, I had been let go systematically from Jefferson Savings because they did not want to pay the maternity leave. My work was impeccable and systems I put into place also aided others in my department (Mortgage Department) in being more efficiently able to prepare documents. I think I was three minutes late one day, after having been late by maybe three to 10 minutes on maybe three or four previous occasions. I was driving from Buckingham to Charlottesville to work which was easily an hour away, and most of the time I was on time. I just reasoned that they didn't want to pay the leave so they used the only thing they could to try and justify terminating me.

So Rashad was the only one working. We had just finished paying for one car that Rashad destroyed by "flying" around the curves of the back roads near my cousin Bruce's house, where we had then been staying. We had just recently bought another car and were making payments. Now money would really be tight. Rashad had been talking about how bored he was with Buckingham and how small town life was about to drive him crazy, and now I was unemployed. We talked about it and decided that moving to DC (where I was born and raised for years) would be a good idea.

The plan was for me to go to DC first and look for a job, since I had relatives there that I could stay with. Then, Rashad and Sheba would come and join me. The plan worked. I worked for George

Washington University's Equal Employment Activities Office in a Senior Secretarial position that I had held before for a summer, which still had the same lawyer and director as when I had worked there before. My boss and director of the department was gracious enough to pull some strings for us or call in a favor and was able to get Rashad a night job in GW's security department, which was ideal because I could work during the day and Rashad could work at night, and we would not need (and did not want) a babysitter.

DC was expensive though, especially to live in the desirable areas. I managed to find a place that could certainly use work, which was in NW (or the North West section of DC). The building was old with high ceilings, which I loved. But the longer we lived there the more we discovered major problems, and housing code violations in the building and apartment. Our daughter, Sheba, threw up her formula when we mixed it with the water there. We had some formula that was pre-mixed and ready to drink, so we didn't make the connection right away that it was the water that was making her sick. We started buying only bottled water in gallon jugs to make her formula.

It wasn't long before I discovered that Rashad could not focus on things sometimes, and seemed to be in his own world. We would call a few friends on the weekends and I would sometimes go over friends' houses when I was feeling up to it. But something wasn't right. I found out exactly what was going on when I came home to find Rashad smoking something out of a glass. I thought he had just found a new way to make a bong to smoke weed from. But I discovered it was crack. I had only seen it once over my college friend, Tony's house when I had tried it. News channels had begun to talk about the substance and how it controlled people and how they couldn't stop using it. There had been a guy named Mike over Tony's, who had shown us the first "crack" we had ever seen. We all smoked weed and had decided to try this "crack". It was pleasant and we liked it, but it was no big deal to me and I could do without it. Since it was already there, I figured, why not? It was downhill from the time we started using it at home. The crack in our neighborhood was stronger than the crack we had over Tony's. I would see to Sheba's needs and feed her, but I began to play with her less and it seemed to me that Rashad never even picked her up anymore.

I had found a new job at a law firm in DC, named Fisher, Wayland Cooper and Leader, which was a great place to work as a Legal Secretary. The salary was great and I was being very sure to provide the best that I could to the partner, David, for whom I worked. Rashad had lost his job (for sleeping on his post) by the time I got this one and would later follow me to Fisher, Wayland. We would have two incomes again and be able to get ahead. But more and more we smoked crack, and pretty soon we were out of control. I can't say what went on in Rashad's head, but I know I had periods that I was terrified of what was going on inside of my body and of how we were not taking care of any of our responsibilities.

Pretty soon I was borrowing money and running a tab at the corner store to make sure that the baby ate. And I was asking the family to pay the rent for us. Somehow, none of what was going on bothered us when we smoked, so we kept smoking. That way we wouldn't have to think about what we were doing and how we looked. After Fisher, Wayland let me go for my extreme tardiness, since we didn't sleep until almost dawn lots of times (they let Rashad go before me), we were evicted from the apartment, mostly because we did not address the issues in court for which we withheld the rent. Before the eviction, Sheba and I had moved back in with my Aunt Stella, hoping that moving there would take us away from the crack. After the eviction, Rashad was there with me and the smoking in the bathroom and laundry room on the lower level began. A few months after being at Aunt Stella's, Alfreda and Leonard, Rashad's sister and brother-in-law visited us suggested that we go to New Jersey and live in Rashad's parents' house and find jobs there. I thought it would be a good idea and would stop us from smoking, especially Rashad who smoked large pieces and never seemed to get enough, and would keep finding ways to get more even when the money was gone and I was trying to sit and relax. But the more I pulled away from using, the more he wanted to do it. I had become afraid of the drug and what it was doing to our lives, but he didn't seem phased at all.

Moving didn't stop our use completely, but it sure cut it back considerably and I was glad about that. We worked for a plastic container factory on different shifts. Someone was always there to take care of the baby. I wanted a skilled position and I applied for other jobs. By the time it looked as though we would be fine and move forward, there was another Michelle in the picture. So I found out some of what Rashad was doing with his time. She had begun to call the house. Then there was that straw that broke the camel's back--she was pregnant, and having a crack baby-by Rashad. I left him and returned to Buckingham where my family was with my baby who was now nearly a year old. About two months after my return, I discovered I was pregnant with my son, Dorian.

When Dorian was born, he looked just like Rashad, with all of his physical family traits. Rashad, his brother Keith and his sister Lisa came to see me in the hospital. They convinced me to go back to New Jersey. Not long after being there, I was able to find a job and before I could start to work, I decided to leave again never to return because he kept bringing crack around me and eventually I was back into active addiction and I did not want to be near it anymore. My Aunt Elaine (for whom I am named) sent me the money for us to come to Buckingham and she sent it in cash after wrapping the money in paper. Rashad intercepted it and smoked it up. We thought someone in the postal service got it, until I later discovered the empty envelope from my aunt in a trunk that stored some of my things. So my brother Alexis and my brother Eric came up to get me, and Rashad and I have not been together since.

I lived in Buckingham in my aunt's basement, which had been HUD approved, supplemental, government-assisted housing. That worked for a while and I got comfortable there. Then it became a burden that I was without a babysitter and stuck at home. I tried babysitting my sister's children as well as my own for income, but they were all very young, close in age to my children, the eldest of whom was Sheba and she was three. They became impossible for me to handle alone, so when I got the opportunity to move to Richmond with my children and seek employment and housing of my own, I took it.

And so began my life in Richmond at my cousin and his girlfriend Wanda's house. The lack of experience or transportation kept me in workplaces below my abilities along with the normal shut-outs because of my race; it was difficult for me to find skilled work. It had been years, and I had not made my first student loan payment, so my credit was really "jacked up". I met Robert when Bruce and Wanda took me to a card game at Lena's (Robert's sister's house). I had my eyes on him right away. Apparently he liked what he saw and wanted to come home with me that night. We exchanged numbers and he called me that night after we returned home. In one of our conversations, Robert told me about a job at Professional Mailers, a mailing services company.

I interviewed there and was hired. It was a minimum wage job, but it was a job and I took it. We worked at the same place so we saw each other every day. Also, while I was at Bruce and Wanda's I met a guy named Caleb who was working outside on the pavement for the complex. We exchanged numbers and Wanda let me use her car to go and see him a couple of times. While Robert was okay, his sister told me that he was in and out of jail, that he had domestic problems in the past and that he did not have a place of his own, so I didn't know if he was a "keeper".

At that time, it was most important that a man would develop a meaningful relationship with me, not rather than what his financial situation was. We could always build together, as I didn't have my own\ place either. The management company for the complex soon gave Caleb an apartment in a complex on the south side of Richmond, and Caleb invited me and the kids to stay with him until I got on my feet. After I and the kids moved in with Caleb, I began to cook and clean and make a home for us. I soon discovered that I didn't care for being on the Southside where we were, not because it was a bad area, but because I had no car and would not be able to get around easily with the kids. I could walk to a bus stop about 5 blocks away in order to catch a bus and get to work. I got a baby sitter just one floor up from us so I could be free to work.

I realized that I enjoyed Robert's company much more than Caleb's and that Caleb was becoming more distant and stranger by the day. One day after work, I went to see Robert's new place and spent some time with him. I didn't want to admit it, but I was beginning to have feelings for Robert that I did not have for Caleb. I went home and discovered that Caleb his friends used crack. He didn't hide it, but rather matter-of-factly told me that crack was something that he did, as though it would be something I would just accept.

A week or so later, I went to Robert's place again and I found myself not wanting to go home. I called Caleb and he said he would pick the kids up. So I stayed longer. Then I discovered that the buses would not be going to the area where I lived and I would have to stay until the early morning hours. When I got home, I got no answer at the door, so I went upstairs to the babysitter's house and she informed me that Caleb had not picked up the children and that she had called the authorities and that my sister had the children.

I later discovered that Caleb had taken the company truck that was afforded him as supervisor and gone south. I would never hear from him again. I would be charged with abandonment of the children unless I completed some program. Apparently, my sister had told the authorities that my "abandonment" was likely related to my marijuana use and I had to go through a center with group sessions and take urinalysis weekly because of my use of marijuana in order to get my kids out of my sister's care and back with me. While I attended those sessions I had to get an apartment of my own. Right then I was living in a room in a rooming house on the North side of town. The program would go on for about 6 months and I sought emergency housing and worked throughout the program.

After a few months, I had public housing in a pretty good spot (if you had to be there), and I was on my own and I didn't know and wouldn't associate with anyone who smoked crack. I was done with crack. I had no problems there in the projects because my apartment was at the corner of the front street of the project and the side street (which was also at the edge of the project).

My new friend Robert came to live with me before my year anniversary there in Fairfield Court. We were like a family. He had something he was going to have to face in court that occurred before we began seeing each other, and he would eventually have to do 6 months in jail, which he did. He was good to have him around the house and he often cleaned the whole house, but he did have some shortcomings. First of all, he did have a habit of coming in late from work, but he wasn't my husband, so I felt I couldn't complain. He helped me out a little bit financially, though he never gave all that he said he would. From time to time we had our spats, and one time it got physical. But since I didn't have any marks that showed, I let it go and we continued with our lives.

Professional Mailers filed for bankruptcy and dismantled and I was again without work. I was at home and looking for work. My cousin Bruce (with whom I and Rashad had stayed in Buckingham, and who I stayed with in Richmond) asked if he could stay with me. Apparently he had left or Wanda had put him out. I told him he could stay and he brought all of his furniture with him. It wasn't long before I discovered through Robert that he was smoking crack in the bedroom. I "went off" on him and told him never to do it again or he would have to leave. Robert had his own problem with crack that he had been working on, and I believed he had been clean for a while. Bruce said he wouldn't smoke in my house again and I believed and trusted him.

A few weeks later Bruce said he had found a place and would be leaving. I got home one day and he had left, so the living room was bare. That would be another bill I would have from one of the furniture rent-to-own places because I would not have an empty living room. Bruce's leaving came at a bad time because I was out of work, but I finally found a part-time job and furnished the living room, but I began to think about using again in my idle time, being continuously frustrated with finding full-time work so that I could move, and get ahead in life, but I did not pick up then. Through a friend, I found out that a contractor had a general maintenance job opening at Phillip Morris. I applied for and got that job and was happy with it, though it was beneath my skills levels, because it was full-time.

I learned the job basics and performed them. The job was in the Research and Development building and I had my own floor to clean, so I was cleaning labs, restrooms and lounge areas. The kids were with me now and I now had to get them up to be on the daycare bus at 6:00am and I had to be on my bus at 6:15 to arrive at work before 7:00am.

Robert had not helped me at all for a few weeks and I realized he may be getting high. After I confronted him with it, he admitted it. There I was trying to figure out how I could get everything paid on the furniture, and phone, rent (based on income) with only food stamps to make it until I got paid from my job. This would be one of the times I asked my family for help, though I don't remember the details. I do know that what I got didn't cover it. I really didn't know anybody, but Robert knew people who would buy food stamps. So I gave him some to sell at 50 cents on the dollar. He came back with some money, and admitted that he had purchased some crack as well. When I said to take it back and get the stamps he laughed. He said they would never take it back and it was a "done deal." That was another fight. At the end of the fight, I just decided that I may as well accept what happened. I let him smoke it since the kids weren't there--and I ended up smoking with him, like a damned fool. I went from there to occasionally smoking. And I went from there to smoking regularly. It just crept up on me. That escape, that good feeling in the midst of problems that would go away and leave you wanting more to bring the feeling back again. I vowed never to spend anything I needed for a bill and I kept that promise. After all, I was solely responsible for the children now.

There was guy at work named John and he was younger than me. He kept coming on to me and I would find him on my floor sometimes watching me. He sat and had lunch with me a few times and we talked. We shared "war stories" about our lives and the troubles we experienced and came to confide in each other about our private lives. One day after work, I stopped by his house near the job. He lived in a high-rise with his mom. And I later discovered that she was just 10 years older than me. She nicknamed him Dickie, a nickname he had most of his life and I used to tease him about it sometimes. We smoked a little weed and things started getting a little hot, but I stopped him because I needed to go and pick the kids up from daycare and I was running late. I knew this situation would arise again because I wanted to be with him.

Robert had been locked up for a while and had been sending me some cards from jail. They were pretty and I could tell he had put some time into making them. I didn't have the heart to destroy them, but I didn't display them either. I still had a soft spot in my heart for

Robert, but I was also glad he was gone with his lies and deceit. It all happened one day when Robert came in from work late (around 10:00pm). For some reason, he pushed me around and then he hit me in my face. I fought back, which was a losing battle, and I yelled at him for hitting me and he kept asking me "what did you just do?". And I just looked at him in disbelief wondering "what the hell is he talking about?" He slumped in a chair, then later went to sleep on the couch. I called the police and had him removed. I was just tired of putting up with him. He already didn't help me with the bills anymore. Now he had the nerve to punch me in my face, and not tell me why. When he went before the judge that next morning for his arraignment, I told the DA to lock his ass up for as long as she could, and then I left. He didn't know how fortunate he was. My first thought was to do as one of my Aunts told me she had done to one of her men decades before now: She said she boiled some sugar and water and threw it on him. I guess I just wasn't *that* mad at him. It wasn't long before I was with Dickie. He also smoked--and so did his mother.

So the vicious cycle continued and I smoked every payday after I paid my bills, got my groceries, and got my bus tickets for the next two weeks. I was the kind of smoker to take care of my bills first because I knew all too well what would happen if I didn't do that first. I really felt like I had a handle on things because I took care of business first, and then what I did was my business. Being in Virginia had taken its toll on me and began to believe that there was nothing more for me than what I had going. Before I got the job I now had, I had looked and looked and found nothing. I never got any skilled job I applied for. I knew about the covert racism in Virginia; I had known it for years. After all, I had gone to high school there and racism was everywhere. No one stopped you from applying for a job. Nor did they deny you an education, but you just were not selected. Made me wish I had been a sciences major in English instead of an arts major, then I could teach, at least. But as it turns out, I majored in English instead of journalism because my school did not offer journalism as a major. It was a highly accredited, predominantly black college and I received an excellent education. But that did not seem to matter and I developed a sense of hopelessness and I used that hopelessness as an excuse to keep getting high. And get high I did whenever I could for years.

Getting high was my escape, my reward to myself. It was the ultimate feeling-- for a few minutes per hit, and I craved it. While I was high nothing mattered, everything was great and I felt good. When I wasn't high I was depressed so I would get high to feel better. The problem came when I could not get high because there were no funds to get high with. I found myself getting crack "on time" and paying when I got paid. I guess my supply would have lasted longer if I didn't share it all the time. I shared mine thinking that my friends would share theirs when I didn't have any-Wrong.

So then I started getting high alone a lot. I became somewhat reclusive and didn't want to see my family when they came. All I wanted to do was get high after I put the kids to bed, hitting with homemade hitters like medicine bottles covered in foil with a makeshift hole in the side and a pen casing extension to pull on. I am not sure when it happened, but I was beginning to become paranoid, wanting to hide whatever I was "hitting" with immediately after the hit. I was beginning to lose weight, but I told myself that it looked good because I could stand to lose about 20 pounds. I thought I had everything on a "down low" and that nobody knew. And for a while I was right.

I had started letting Dickie come around and had started spending my time at home with him. Sexually, he was great, and he could relate to me on many levels, but still had some immature ways about him and was nearly ten years younger. Our job lost the contract because my supervisor had been caught taking cases of cigarettes from the job and selling them to support his habit. I knew that he smoked crack because he smoked on the job, and Robert and I had bought crack from him a couple of times. I had even made the mistake of smoking with him on the job one day and I swore I would never do that again because I could hardly complete my day and was paranoid all day. Anyway, not long after it was determined that Vernon was the ring leader in the cigarette capers, he was fired and incarcerated. Then our company was underbid by another company and we were all without jobs.

Not long after that, my Aunt Elaine came to Richmond and asked me if the children could come to live with her. Since I had no baby sitter and could no longer pay for daycare, I let them go. It was temporary, just until I could get a job, I told myself. I spent more and more time with Dickie and his mom just getting high and it wasn't long before we were into buying and selling crack and marijuana. I wanted to sell heroin because I knew I wouldn't use it. But, our people wanted us to sell the "big sellers" with the greatest turn around in profit. I did well with this for a while, and was able to pay my bills and smoke. As I became known for my street vending, I got bigger profits and bigger "rocks". Thankfully, I just worked within our little sect.

One day, it all fell apart and our supplier was taken down. If we didn't smoke so much, we would have been able to go into business for ourselves. But as it turned out, we smoked ourselves down to nothing. The rent-to-own people had come to get their belongings and I avoided them as long as I could, then sold a lot of their stuff and reported it stolen. My home actually did get robbed on another occasion while I was hanging out with Dickie and his mom, and I am still wondering if Dickie left my back door open to let someone in. I remember that he would not bring me home when I thought about the door possibly being unlocked, and that he did not seem surprised when I did return home to a nearly empty house. For some reason I had always trusted the men I was with to "have my back" when they needed to. I never expected that I was being played by Dickie because I was always with him. In retrospect, and with the added learning I now have, I was just a vehicle for him to get what he wanted. He wanted a place to retreat, a female at his disposal (for sexual purposes) and another place to get high without his mother. I provided all three.

My life was falling apart and I felt like I didn't have anyone. Both of my children were with my Aunt Elaine and I had no one where I was in Richmond who cared anything for me except Dickie. After losing my things, Dickie helped me to get some things from an abandoned house to furnish my house. I also took some attractive lawn furniture to furnish my living room. The furnishings were actually nice and since I had no income, I had no rent. So, I reasoned that I was okay. I thought I would go crazy sometimes when I wasn't with Dickie, because it was then that I thought about my situation and how I had nothing and had very little coming in. The reason I let the kids go with my aunt was to get on my feet, and I wasn't moving forward. Dickie and I also smoked up most of our unemployment checks, both with and without his mother, who had a boyfriend, Richard who spent as well. She could just blow him her smoke and he was satisfied. Not so for me and Dickie.

One night, while Dickie and I were trying to figure out how we would get our next hit, I thought about the fact that an old guy, whose house I went over to whenever I was doing laundry to drink would be out of town. Double A was his nickname. He had told me that he would be out of town for a few days (he was a truck driver). I told Dickie that he wouldn't be home but that I was not going to go inside his house, but he could go in, and that we might be able to get enough items to sell or we might even be able to find some money. That was it. We were going to break into Double A's apartment, get some stuff and go. I had no idea that night would change my life forever.

Double A had one of those locks that needed a key on the inside and outside. The only way in would be through a window. Dickie broke the window and the neighbors heard it. I expected him to go in after people around his apartment settled down, but he had a different plan. He wanted to give me a boost to go in and start handing things out to him. As soon as I got in and unplugged the television, I heard sirens and was about to go back out of the window when I saw flashlights. I ducked back in. Damn, how had I let Dickie talk me into this?! I looked to the front of the apartment and I saw flashlights there, too. That was it, I was trapped. The police instructed me to stay where they could see me and to put my hands over my head until they could get a key from the landlord. I tried to lie and say Double A had left me there, but when they asked to see the bottom of my sneakers and the wetness and grass there, I understood why they had asked me to do that and I knew it was over. I was so mad at Dickie, who had disappeared after insisting that I go in rather than leave it alone like I tried to do, especially after we had alerted the neighbors.

My only way out was to make a deal, because it was clear I was going down. I made a statement before going downtown so that the lieutenant would get the magistrate to let me go on my own recognizance so that I could come home and call my family. My family would have no understanding of how I came to such a pass. And I didn't know how to tell them, but I had to. They would never understand and I was scared. I had never been in any legal trouble in my life. None of us had. The worst trouble I had ever been in was for a traffic ticket, and I had only ever had one of them in my 33 years. I had no idea what the right way was to handle the situation. All I knew was that if I made a statement, I would be let go for now. They asked me where the man was that was out there with me. I reasoned, why should I protect him, when he left me here to take the fall alone? So I sent them to my house and told them that the back door was open (I left it that way for our return.) I never saw him but before I was released the police said they had Dickie in custody.

In the "wee hours of the morning", I walked home from downtown and thought about my children and how I needed them so much right now, but how I couldn't take care of them. I prayed for the first time in a very long time, asking Allah for his mercy and provision, to do for me what I was unable to do for myself. When I got home I would call Aunt Elaine and try to figure out how to tell her about the mess I was in. Should I tell her about the drugs or try to hide that fact? Would the whole family disown me if they knew? I had to tell her. I had to tell somebody. I couldn't go on not having an outlet except for other people who sold and used drugs. I wanted to stop, but I couldn't because I couldn't deal with my feelings when I was sober for any length of time. Reality would come storming in and when I finished looking at myself and looking at my situation, I was reduced to nothing and I didn't want feel that way.

When I got home I rested a while, then asked my next door neighbor if I could use her phone. I remember calling and telling Aunt Elaine that I was in trouble, that I had been arrested and released on my own recognizances. I would have to appear in court on the date that the magistrate gave me. I told her that I was doing drugs and I blamed Dickie for leading me to commit a crime that was classified as a felony in order to get more drugs. I fell apart on the phone crying and confessing everything I had done, relieved to finally be able to tell somebody I loved and who loved me. She wanted me to "come home", but I did not see the point if I was to come to court soon. But I knew that if I didn't go home, I would wallow in self-pity and continue to find ways to keep using. For a while I stayed in my apartment and weighed my options. I remembered how I wanted to make it on my own, even with my children. When I accepted the project apartment, I told myself that I wouldn't be there long, that I was going to make it out because I was going to find an opportunity.

Every time I saw an ad that seemed to offer me the opportunity to make a decent income, it was always out of reach (outside of the mass transportation system). What I got was always menial and beneath my skills levels, and I accepted the work because it was work. It was income and it was better than nothing, I reasoned. But this, committing a crime, I would never live down with my family.

Until I married and left Virginia for DC with Rashad, I had been held in the same light as my other brothers and sisters who had graduated from college. I now felt that my brothers and sisters would shun me and not support me because no one else in the family had ever done anything like this. We were educators and professionals and higher on the "totem pole" than the average family. They would say that I had been stupid and would not understand how I ended up in such a condition. So I hid what I did from my family and believed that I could work it out. I had smoked weed, PCP, dropped acid and I still achieved undeterred, but crack was a whole new and different monster, fierce and uncontrollable after time. And the evidence that I used crack was now going to be clear.

I wanted to go home, but I didn't want to face my family and their questions. I supposed that Aunt Elaine had gone ahead and told the family. But I would go home and I would work on my problem. Rashad had gone into the army and had come to Richmond once to visit me and the children. When he came, I introduced him to his son whom he had not seen since he was around 6 months old. Dorian was now 2 ½ or 3years old. I called Dorian downstairs and said "You know how I told you that Pooh Bear (Robert) was not your father and that you father's name was Ivory?" Dorian said, "yes". I said "This is Ivory". Dorian hid himself behind me after showing us a look of disbelief. He didn't want to go to Ivory because he didn't know him. He eventually came out from behind me and asked Rashad (Ivory) if he was really his father, and where he had been. Anyway, since Rashad was in the Army, he had medical insurance for all of us. So I sought treatment at Charter Westbrook, a treatment center for the Richmond area, which was an in-house treatment center. I was to be there at least 30 days and I was to have family therapy sessions after being there maybe a couple of weeks.

There was an indoor pool and other recreational facilities as well as a ceramic shop, both of which I utilized. We had group sessions and I actually gained weight. Close to the end of the 30-day stay, I learned that I could stay for an extended period of time, which I felt I could benefit from. It required a family group session in which my problems could be discussed and a plan of action could be made. I still believe today that some of the things that my sister said caused my stay not to be continued. I don't remember exactly what she said, but I remember defending myself, and that she just denied that I had the problems that I said caused my use, that I was just using because I wanted to use and that none of the causes that I said contributed to my use were real.

I guess she just didn't know what I was going through and because of our spats, stemming from a sibling rivalry we had because she knew I was my father's favorite, overruled any consideration she could have about the trials I had undergone. She just believed I was being a brat and just wanted to use. I can't prove she was the cause, but I know that all considerations about an extended stay were halted and I was released days later. I felt then that she hated me. She didn't know that while she was fighting me as a child that I was lost. I was not the aggressor that she was. And the way daddy was, an alcoholic, which we understood as children, she could have had his favor because I didn't want it. I feared him more than anything and did not feel Mom or Dad were emotionally there for me. Mom wasn't there because she constantly had to fight Dad because of his drinking. Perhaps she needed to feel loved, and I know I didn't feel loved by Dad and Mom wasn't always free to show me love because of what she went through regularly. I felt that I was just there. So I found activities to occupy my time, so I wouldn't have to be home.

When I had my little sister at home, I felt like I had purpose in leading and teaching her, but when she was given to Aunt Elaine and

Uncle Ernest to raise, I didn't feel like I had much purpose anymore. My little sister had been my best friend. We did everything together, and I treated her the way I wished Dru treated me. I used to strike out at Dru by saying horrible things to her to hurt her as much as she hurt me. They were things that I wish now that I could take back. Maybe I deserved what she said in that family session, I reasoned, and I just let it go at that, thinking that stuffing how I felt away, would make it go away, which was what I had learned to do all my life. If it didn't kill you, I was taught, you got over it and you moved on.

That's how it was when I was either molested, or nearly molested by my father when we lived on Brooks Street when I was in kindergarten. Mom banged on the door, made him open it and promised to kill him if he ever tried it again, and he never did. But I still believe that he allowed Pee Wee to molest me some years later. Otherwise how did I wake up on the living room floor with him and his hand in my panties and end up over his house to babysit where he tried it again while I was wide awake? Dru could have Dad and I would gladly let her have any affection he had to give. I was scared to death of him. All that I said to hurt her, and all the stuff I did to get her in trouble was because she was always fighting me. And since I could never win the fight, since she was so much bigger and stronger, I got her in other ways. I guess I never stopped to consider just how messed up she had to feel behind the trouble I got her in and the lack of favoritism she got. All I felt was lost and alone. Even then she was strong, and I felt weak.

I never forgot the day that Dad had Mom on the floor in the living room fighting her and she saw me and said "Go and get the police". I was on my way. I was going to go to Uncle Frank's house and call because he lived in the court across the street. But as I was headed to the door, Dad said "if you go out that door, I'll kill you." I froze in my tracks. If looks could kill, I would have died in that moment looking at his angry piercing eyes as they glared at me. Something died in me that day, something else innocent and trusting, and it paralyzed something in me that I have never gotten back--something I can feel but cannot pinpoint that has to do with my fluid, natural movement from one action to the next, which is something I now manage, but not nearly as well as before that moment--even today.

Here I was about to go home now. I would go first to Buckingham to visit. Then I would return to my place. Not long after returning to my place, I got a "Pay-Or-Quit". This time I didn't know if I even wanted the place or not. I doubted if I would get any assistance from anyone under the circumstances. I contacted Dickie and decided to try and make the money with him that I would need to pay my rent. I didn't really understand the importance of truly changing the 'people, places and things' to remain clean and sober, because this was my first treatment. At the time, had I been honest with myself, I would have realized that I wasn't necessarily glad to be free from my addiction. Right then, I really could stand to be high because I would forget about my upcoming court date and problems with my apartment.

As it turned out, I was losing the apartment faster than I thought, and since everybody wanted me to come back to Buckingham, nobody was going to help me keep the apartment. And lose it, I did. I went to Buckingham for a while and tried to plan a course of action. But I knew I needed to be back in Richmond to find work and meet with my attorney before appearing in court. So I asked my sister if I could stay at her house for a while and she agreed. It was in that stay that I learned that my sister Dru and I could not live in the same dwelling for any significant period of time. There was something that bugged the hell out of her about me and vice versa.

One day while she was at work, I decided to get it touch with Dickie. I met him at the old spot on Midlothian Turnpike, where we often sold drugs. His mother was also there at Aunt JoAnn's. For some reason that I did not understand, I was drawn to Dickie, regardless of what we had just gone through, what he just put me through. I felt like I needed him, and I couldn't control that need, I needed to be with him. Was it because I felt whole with him or that I needed to fill a hole in me? No matter what I had to be with him. Was it because the sex was good, that I felt secure with him? Dickie and I got into a fight that night and I ended up going to the hospital in an ambulance. While in the ambulance, I started to wonder just how I would get back to where Dickie was when I was done in the emergency room. It was a misunderstanding and Dickie didn't let me talk so that I could explain what happened in the bathroom. I truly wasn't what it looked like: We hadn't been having sex, we had just been smoking. Once he understood, we would be okay again. He never would have hit me if he wasn't so hurt. He had never done that before. It was just a fluke, it wouldn't happen again.

Anyway, I would have to find a way back from the suburban hospital back to where Dickie was somehow. I couldn't call my sister, not after sneaking away. She would ask me thousands of questions, and I didn't want to answer any of them. I would be ashamed to answer any of them. I thought then that my situation would look to her like something it was not, that she would never understand what was actually going on inside of me, and for whatever reason, being with Dickie was making it all better. I had somebody to be close to, to hold me and that was a comfort for me, the only comfort or peace other than the total escape of getting high. I knew God existed and that there was a path to him that I didn't really know. But someday, I always knew, I would find the path and write my book.

I knew I would be shown everything I needed to know in order to finish it at some point in my life, and straighten out my path and complete my story, record it and help many. But I had to get past my current condition and get set on the right path to some kind of financial progress. There was one problem: I never had a long term success at anything, and I was going down fast, with no knowledge of how to turn it around. For one thing, Virginia was still covertly very racist, perhaps more racist than most states in the nation. I seemed to have better luck getting jobs before my college education than after college education in Virginia. Everything I found was out of reach via mass transportation, and I had no car, or I was never called back after an interview. But I kept working menial jobs with minimal pay, hoping things would change and an opportunity would come along that utilized my skills.

But for now I needed to get back to Dickie. After resting as instructed and being examined, I set my feet to walking back towards Midlothian Turnpike, knowing the task would be impossible without a ride, which I hoped to hitchhike at some point during my walk. I grew tired rather quickly, perhaps because of my injuries. I got some yells out of the windows of passersby calling me names and making comments about me walking in their neighborhood. The last comment was more of a threat about what would happen to me if I was still there when they turned around and came back my way. I believed them because they had thrown a few objects at me. I wished that I had called my sister to come and get me. I ran towards a building on my right that was locked. I was going to hide, so I went around the back of the building, but could not get in. I broke a window in the basement and went into the building, afraid. Not long after that I heard voices outside and I hid in a room in the closet of what seemed to be the copy room in a dentist's office. I must have tripped a silent alarm because moments later the police came into the room and I was actually relieved. That is, until I discovered that I would be charged with trespassing and locked up again.

This time I had a small bond and had violated the terms of the recognizance bond. My family would never get me out although I would later call from jail. It was as simple as the fact that I wanted to do what I wanted to do and not deal with my sister. I made the choice to go where Dickie was and now I was going back to jail. I felt stupid and helpless.

By the time I saw my lawyer, I had done a couple of weeks in jail. I remember us going over the presentencing report and seeing that it provided points for whether or not I had served time for a crime ever before and on the lawyer's prepared copy there were no points in that section, but when I did the 30 days for the trespass, I had served time for a crime. I guessed that my lawyer knew what he was doing so I didn't say anything. Not saying anything to him came back to haunt me when I went to court about the trespass charge and the Commonwealth Attorney noted that I had served time for another crime and that made it appear that my lawyer was trying to deceive the court on my behalf, which resulted in my conviction and sentencing to 10 years with 6 years suspended on the breaking and entering. People in jail had told me that each year you get when convicted of a felony at that time represented 2 months that you would have to serve.

I wasn't going home like my lawyer had me believing based on the presentencing report, because after the additional points, the recommendation was now incarceration. I was looking at 8 months minimally. When the judge sentenced me to 4 years, he said "in a state facility", which inmates later told me meant that I would have to "touch state ground" before I was released. That meant I would be going to one of the women's prisons in the state before I was released. I was just devastated because I expected to go home that day with probation. I was unresponsive when I was asked questions about why I was back and how much time I got. I got on my bunk and just laid there looking up at the fan in the ceiling. I felt disoriented. How could I possibly be there that long? What would I do? What did people who went to jail do with their time? I felt like the life had been snatched out of me.

Once I went through my emotional thing and accepted that I wasn't going anywhere for quite a while, I was able to see past my shock and dismay at coming back to jail. I became the seamstress one day when over the PA system the question was asked about whether or not anyone could sew. I had to be led out of the cell block to a sewing machine. If I could thread the old machine, I had the job. I threaded it and every day, I had a job and I would make little to nothing, but it was something constructive to do and would get me off the cell block.

With the overcrowding I had just gotten a bottom bunk and began to settle into what would be my lifestyle for a while. I met this guy named Larry (nicknamed "Jo Jo") in the jail library, which was next to the commissary window. He was a bright spot in my days there in jail. He is an artist and so the envelopes he sent always had beautiful artwork on them. He also took the time to make elaborate cards that he sent me, which were the envy of most females on the block. They paid me to have him make cards and he made them gladly at no cost to me. We exchanged every thought, every experience including sexual ones. His letters made my day. He made me necklaces with charms formed like horns just like the ones on real jewelry. They would always be different colors and I always thought they were pretty. I wore them proudly. I began to see how people actually got hooked up in jail and began to feel for the people they communicated with by letter. I guess it was a great time to allow feelings to flow-- with a clear head.

Time and effort and especially emotions went into these "jailhouse romances". I don't think I ever communicated so deeply with a man except in that jail setting. I came to depend on the communication and the artwork from Larry. I knew he felt the same way. With this relationship, we knew we had someone to care about us, someone who understood and did not judge us for what we had done. Our letters from each other helped to sustain us. And they gave us a sense of loyalty to each other, a bond through which we shared our secrets, the most confidential details of our lives, our sexuality and our hopes for the future.

This form of a "relationship" was essential to me in my incarceration. It was like having an "outside connection" away from the drab of the women's prison I was in. Even though he, too was incarcerated, Larry's surroundings were different and so was his experience because he was a man. I promised Larry that he would do the artwork for my book. (I can't reach him now, but my second edition will bear his artwork.) In a place where you are nothing but a number to those in authority, it was essential for me to feel that someone of the opposite sex understood and cared about me, my thoughts and ideas, my aspirations. It was validation and it was calming to my spirit.

I continued to work as the seamstress in the jail, and in my repair of the jail uniforms, I put flowers on the women's patches and X's on the men's patches (for Malcolm X) to cover the torn places on the "good" uniforms by making patches from "scrap" uniforms.

One night at 11:00, when court dates and transfers came across the PA system, they called my name and said "bag and baggage" which meant that the next day I would be transferred to a state facility for women. It hardly seemed like I had enough time left to serve to be transferred. But one of two things had occurred before the announcement: When I was sentenced, the Judge used the language "in a state facility" and everybody told me that meant I would have to "touch state ground" or go to a women's state prison before I completed my sentence. I had also had a disagreement with one of the Captains in authority at Richmond City Jail, and she could have forced the transfer.

I wondered how I would contact my family. I wrote letters that night to my children and to Larry to tell them I was being moved and that I would tell them where as soon as I could send them the next letter. I said my goodbyes to my friends on the tier and in the morning I would find out while in route what my destination was. I saw the wisdom then of not letting us know about transfers until after the phones were turned off. Everybody would not be like me and just want to notify people who cared that I was moving to another facility. Some of the inmates had told me that being in a state facility was better that being in the city jail. I hoped so.

When I got to Goochland, I realized that there were no fences like I had expected and neither were there any gates when entering the facility. I would later learn that the person who had owned the land had donated it only on the condition that there were never any fences or gates on the facility itself. Instead of there being one big building, there were several buildings for housing, each one like a residence hall of sorts. The building I was to start in, along with all other new comers, was in the medical hall.

I would first have to wash my hair and body with a shampoo for lice. Then I would have a complete physical and be placed on the second floor of that building in a room with one other inmate. I was given the codes of conduct and violations/penalties for guidelines for all inmates. It was a long hall consisting of about 20-30 rooms on either side of the hall. For count (done 3 times daily) we had to stand on either side of the door to our rooms.

Each building had a counselor that we all had to meet with and we had the option to visit the prison psychiatrist if we thought we needed medication or counseling to make it through our sentence, especially if we needed it at the jails we came from. We had a choice of jobs but would not be able to work until we were moved to general population. Even then we would have to start out in the laundry @ .23 cents per hour. We would have to be recommended to go to better jobs like keypunch at .45 cents per hour. Commissary was only once a month and you had to get all you could pay for then.

For some reason, we went on lockdown and could not even get commissary for weeks. In that time everybody's cigarette supply was gone or nearly gone, and we got a little frantic. I hadn't heard from Larry, and I could not make phone calls until my numbers were in the system (we had to do a phone list and submit it to all the numbers we would call, and we could not call anyone who was not on the list we turned in). I sent a letter to my sister and inside of it, I had a stamped letter to Larry. I sent the letter to her because we were not allowed to communicate with inmates in other facilities. I understood the concept, but I wasn't plotting and neither was Larry. We had to communicate to keep up our morale. I asked my sister if she would forward my letters for me. Since she had a post office box she could send it out whenever she went to the post office. She sent it for me and it wasn't long before I got a letter back. Apparently, they had moved Larry too. Larry had given me his home address and I sent his mom a letter also, asking her to get it to Larry. By the time I had been moved to Hall 6, I had gotten a letter from Larry. I was so relieved. Everything was alright again.

I was first assigned the work detail of 2 kitchen. That means that the kitchen of the hall I went to when I first got to Goochland (Hall 2) would be where I worked until I was eligible to go to the laundry. I mostly washed pots and pans. Apparently the person who was the dishwasher was released from the prison and dishwashing was passed on to the new person in the kitchen. If we got another person assigned to the kitchen, I could then move to preparing some of the food. The food was very rich there and the portions were sizable. We got to eat all that we wanted to, we just couldn't take anything out of the kitchen. We prepared meals for the people in C custody, who had the most serious crimes and the most severe behavioral problems. All we had to do was prepare their covered trays and send the food over 20 trays at a time. The unit only housed maybe 40 people. We could hear their cries at night. Some said that abuse went on in that building and that being "in the hole", on the lower level meant that you used a toilet that was just a hole in the floor. I don't know how true that is, but I know the cries were very real--and loud. I could hear them well at night when I was in 2 Hall, but not in 6 Hall's 1st level, where the living space I was in was like a barracks, with beds in a row on both sides of the wall and a hallway down the middle. I would be transferred from here to my permanent room when it became available.

I had decided that I would not get close to anyone and just do my time and stay focused on what I had to do to be sure to make "first parole", which is a term for making parole the first time you go before the board. We knew the easiest way to blow parole was to have major infractions on your institutional record. My whole time there I had only one, which was for being in an unauthorized area (someone else's room). I saw the "snitch" when she went to the officer's desk to report me. I had gone in to get a few cigarettes. I almost got another major infraction for "disobeying a direct order", which was a Class A major infraction, but other inmates talked me down from my fury and I just sat down. CO Woods was really lucky that day that I had people (other inmates) who were on my side and were sensible enough to anticipate what would happen if I acted out what I was feeling. I was glad they cared enough not to want to see me do additional time, even though some of their sentences were lengthy. None of these inmates seemed to be bad people, we had all just made some very bad choices. Perhaps I would make a few friends before leaving after all.

Another month went by and I was moved to my permanent Hall and now I worked in the laundry. My request for keypunch was also being processed. I met with the representative for the parole board and was approved for parole. I awaited my release date. I was released one day in November which marked just over a year that I had been incarcerated. I had one year supervised parole to look forward to, during which time I would need to report to my parole officer each month, undergo urinalysis and find work.

I was paroled to a half-way house of sorts, which was an old mansion in an affluent area in Richmond. Not just parolees lived there. Students and women from all walks of life lived there as well and they worked their way back into society and into self-sufficiency. Since I knew no people there, I went to visit my old neighborhood in Churchill.

I met a guy named James that I had met not long before my incarnation at a party. He had lost a lot of weight and was in Richmond to stay with his mother. I was at the bootlegger's house around the corner from where I had lived before being incarcerated. She was elderly, but she still managed to make her money. She bought the cheapest liquor and gave the biggest drinks for .50 cents each. Three of her dollar drinks could put you on your behind. Her elder sister stayed there as well, and they had relatives that lived in the two houses next to hers. Anyway, James and I talked. I learned that his nickname was "Big Stuff" and I laughed when I first heard the name. He bought me a couple of drinks and a couple of beers and I met his son and reunited with others that I knew as they came by. By the time I was about to return home for the evening, it was clear that James really liked me and others there told me that he had liked me since the first time he saw me a year or two earlier. We exchanged numbers and I promised to call him when I had made it home safely.

I continued to look for work which was a condition of my parole. In the meantime, the house operations manager offered me a job as a cook in the kitchen there at the Inn. I wouldn't get paid, but it would take care of my keep and I would not have to pay to be there. I was very stressed about my financial situation and I began to lose my motivation after trying repeatedly to find work and just ending up with the job in the kitchen where I lived. I began to question whether I would ever find work again or if my criminal record would forever eliminate any opportunities in the oppressive Virginia.

I found myself cooking dinner and then leaving to go and see James. It wasn't long before I learned that James got high. If I remember correctly, when I got to his mom's house one day, we went to a lady's house that he knew where he pulled out the smoke and offered me some. And what did I do? I got high too, of course. I should have had my fill of pain and humiliation, but I wanted the high. At least I would forget about how I felt about myself and my life for a while and just have a good time. And at least I didn't have to pay for it this time--not out of my pocket, that is.

There was a pay phone on each floor. So, of course, we had to pay to use it or use the office phone where others could be privy to your conversation. Sometimes I would look for work in the mornings, but most of the time I just waited for James to call me and make plans to see him after cooking. I took items from the Inn for resale like food items and personal items like soaps and lotions that were there for the Inn members and James, and I resold them to get high. I guess I just wasn't finished using cocaine and alcohol to suppress my feelings. Whenever I didn't use, I thought about all that was wrong with my life. I missed my children and I couldn't go and get them because I had no place for them to stay. I felt useless, helpless. I couldn't help feeling that there was no way out. Getting high didn't fix my situation, but it did help me to cope with my unfruitful life. I often talked to my brother, Eric and my Aunt Elaine. Sometimes I didn't want to talk to my children because I didn't want to have to answer their question "When are you coming to get us?" I felt like it would take a miracle to get another apartment. When I went to interviews, I always knew that my record would shut me out of anything that was not menial labor. The minute I said I had been convicted of a felony, I knew it was over. And I may as well admit that I had a record because they would check anyway. I couldn't even vote or get another apartment under the public housing sector anymore. I learned back in 1980 that giving up would solve nothing. I had to keep fighting and somehow I would make it. I was tired of asking my family for money, especially since they would need to know what I needed the money for and I would have to go into long explanations. I supposed that their questions were warranted because of the history I had. But I never asked them for anything unless I did exactly what I said I was going to do with the money. Somehow, I felt that Allah would not bless me if I did or would penalize me for it. And whatever I did, I would never steal from my family because they were all that I had. Losing my family would literally kill me. Nothing would fix that--not even using.

James and I became quite an item and the people in the neighborhood knew it, and they teased us while we just smiled. Going to James' mother's house became my new priority as I settled into just being the cook at the Inn until early evening and then going to be with James. Whenever I didn't go to be with him, he called, and once or twice he came to get me. I guessed that he was just as dependent upon me as I was upon him.

We would smoke when we could. He had told me that he had health problems. He was a diabetic and had undergone surgery. He made the statement one day that his doctor had told him that if went out and started smoking again it would kill him. Apparently, when he smoked before he smoked in large volumes, according to the stories he told me. I asked him why he smoked now and he said he wanted to. He didn't believe what the doctor told him and said if smoking was going to kill him he would already be dead. So he continued to smoke. One day he called me and told me he had sold a big air conditioner and to come over as soon as I could because he had something for me. He had gone over the lady's house where we smoked sometimes and they had been smoking before I got there.

He saw me as I approached his mother's house because he was standing inside the doorway of that lady's house. Apparently I was too late and the smoke was gone, but he said he had something else in the works. His mother had gone out, so we watched tv when we returned to her house. I remember that Twilight Zone, the Movie was on and James was in the kitchen. I looked up and he was in the floor in the kitchen. His eyes were closed. I called 911 and I called out his name, "Big Stuff! Big Stuff!", but he didn't answer. I tried performing CPR. By the time the EMT's got there only minutes had passed, but they said he was gone, though they kept working on him.

His mother and brother returned and I stayed to let them know what was going on. James was never revived. His sister was there from Maryland and she said it was his time, that he knew what he was doing and what the consequences were. I was devastated. I called the Inn and let them know what happened and that it would likely be very late before I got home. And it was. When I finally got home, I was in a daze. This was incredulous to me, and my world was turned upside down. The family asked me to write a piece to go into the program and I did. They liked it.

At the funeral I talked with his mother who knew how I felt about James, but more importantly, knew how he felt about me. After the funeral, I overheard one of his brothers blaming me for his death. I went over to the lady's house where he had been smoking because I didn't know anywhere else to go and I had to get out of his mother's house. I was crying as I told her what was going on. She knew he had passed because I told her that night. She told me that James said that he had carried this air conditioner from an abandoned house for quite a few blocks and sold it. She said that he was having some trouble while he was smoking and was about to leave when he saw me from her doorway. In a way I was glad that I had not been there that day. But in another sense I think I might have stopped him from smoking and walked him home, and he might still be alive.

Soon his sister came toward the porch where we were sitting and called me back to the house. She told me not to feel bad and that James knew better. That he was a grown man and nobody held a gun to his head. He made the choice. I told her that I was not with him when he was smoking, that it was over when I got there. She said it didn't matter. She said she knew he loved me and she didn't want me to feel the way that I did. So I rejoined the family. I drank a lot of alcohol that day and I cried a lot. I finally got home and fell asleep still dressed.

Management at the Inn knew that I had lost my friend and I didn't have to work for the next few days. They offered me counsel, but I just went back to the neighborhood in Churchill and reminisced about what we used to do. I went to both of the bootlegger's houses that we went to and got drinks on the house so that I could drown myself in my troubles. I also continued to go and see James' mother when I wasn't "drowning" and stayed until 9 or 10 o' clock in the evening the way I did when James was there.

After a couple of months, I went to her house less and less, but I called every day for a long time. I had to because I had to have a connection with James until I could get through my grief.

Chapter 10 (1993)

I continued to live at the Inn and cook. One day a new member came to live at the Inn named Bonnie. She would be in the room next to mine and she told me that there were openings at Morrison's Cafeteria. I went and applied and started out at the register in front of the Restaurant. I was told when I was hired that I would also be utilized as a cook when the need arose, that they had recipes for everything that we should never reveal. I worked the register for months with another lady and all was well. Bonnie and I would get our checks and go to places she was familiar with and smoke. We had an 11 o'clock curfew that we kept breaking and we were asked to move after taking our keys failed to get us in on time.

I went to Margaret's house and asked if I could stay with her until I got my pay check. I said that I would give her money for being there on payday. She had squatters on the couch from time to time, so I hoped it was okay. It was, and I moved most of my things into the storage space out back and slept on the couch. There was a corner store across the street, and I talked to the lady that lived over the store about staying with her. I helped her pay her rent, so she let me stay and the owner said it was okay for us to share the apartment. The lady was overweight and she was on an oxygen tank, yet she still smoked cigarettes. As you can imagine, she didn't last long. One day when I returned from work she had died. Now I was alone in the apartment.

Bonnie came by sometimes and, as usual we would do a little getting high and buy a few drinks from across the street. I never really had to food shop because I could live off of the leftovers I brought home from the job. So I only had the rent, which was a large portion of my income.

I had met a guy named Mike at work who was the dishwasher by choice. He had been a cook but preferred washing the dishes because he could work at his own pace and not have to be bothered by others. He was handsome and stocky with one little grey patch in his hair and I used to imagine what it would be like to be with him. He also flirted with me daily and I knew I would eventually be with him. We took our lunch breaks together and talked, getting to know each other. Sometimes we ate at Morrison's and sometimes we walked just across the lot to Friday's and ate and had cocktails. After a couple of months, I invited him over. That is when I learned that he also smoked 'crack'. We smoked that night, but not a lot. Our focus that night was to be with each other sexually and it was good. I knew that I was just filling the hole that James left in my life but I needed to feel close to a man. I didn't understand why that was, I just knew that it was. Mike and I continued to see each other and to keep our relationship as separate from the job as we could, until one day when my parole officer came to the job. I hadn't been in to see him because I knew I wasn't clean and that he might do a drug screening.

Mike took over for me at the prep table while I went out to meet with him. My parole officer told me that I was expected to come to see him the next day or he would issue a warrant for my arrest. So I went the next day, and he told me that my previous drug screen was positive and that he suspected that if he gave me one then, it would be positive as well. A police officer came into his office and put a cuff on one arm while I was still sitting. And off to jail I went. I could get released earlier than expected if I went into in-house drug treatment. I decided to accept the condition, so from jail, I would go to an in-house drug treatment center. After a month in the facility, I would be allowed to return to work, if my job would accept me back.

The job accepted me back and I caught buses to work and arranged transportation through Mike to get back from work.

One of the first things I noticed after settling in my room with my roommate, Barbara was that I knew someone who worked there. Maurice had been my boyfriend about 15 years back. He ran the kitchen. I remembered when he worked at Lum's and I attended VCU for a semester or two right after high school and we met. We began a relationship, then I started working at Lum's for a while too. He recognized me and I recognized him and we spoke. I discovered he was getting married soon and I stepped back. When I thought about it, I really didn't want to be with him because we had a dysfunctional relationship and I didn't need to restart a bad relationship.

We never did anything but smoke weed and drink. We had an occasional snort of a little coke, and I do mean little and I mean occasional like "hardly ever." He had stayed with me for a while in some housing near campus. But he had a room on the other side of Broad Street. It is just that mine was much nicer and the best choice to be together in comfort. I had only lived there months before going home to my parents' house. The last thing dad told me was "You can always come home." The funding was not there for me to finish at VCU and my grades were shot because I knew I couldn't stay anyway. So, I spent more time having fun than going to class, and most of that "fun" I had with him.

The other "fun" was with my friend Dolly E. She was from Harlem and we had the same major. I had met her in passing and she lived in the extended student housing which was rooms in brownstones. She started seeing this guy named Wilbur B. He and his brothers were pretty popular around campus for providing entertainment in clubs and private parties by "DJing." It wasn't long before I brought Maurice and his "road dog" Charles around.

I later spent some time in Harlem with Dolly and it was everything I hoped it would be and more. Dolly showed me around and we went everywhere while I was there: It was 1977 and it was hot outside. We went to Manhattan, Brooklyn, the Bronx. We went to clubs like Club 371 and Small's Paradise. When we went to Long Island, we went to a club that was more like an old theater with three levels that were likely balcony areas back in the day, but now were large openings divided by columns and dance floors. It was the largest such event I had ever been to besides the Earth, Wind and Fire concert at the Coliseum. And according to Dolly, it was this "new thing" in music that was starting up and gaining popularity in the boroughs of New York, especially Harlem.

It was a show with Grandmaster Flash and the Furious Five, Kool Herc and Melle Mel. All I knew was it was the best music I had ever heard and that I had never heard anything like it. People there knew all that was about to be said and they followed along. It was amazing and I saw that show as an example of how New York was different from any place I had ever been. Even though most of New York, especially Harlem was still torn up like a lot of cities, as a result of the riots, it was still the most awesome trip I had ever taken. I made a scrapbook that I kept for years.

Anyway, whenever Maurice and I spoke, we spoke of the pleasant times we had back in the day and about where our lives had gone since. Both of our stories had good and bad events in them. He and I both knew that we didn't want to venture into a relationship ever again. So we didn't even talk about that at all.

I was smart enough to know what I should say while in the program, but deep down inside I knew that I wasn't clean because I wanted to be clean, I was clean because they made me be clean. Being high helped me to cope and I wasn't ready to let it go. Getting high felt good and when I was high, I didn't think about any of the conflicts in my life and getting high also suppressed my need and desire to be with my children and helped me not to feel so bad about not being there for them.

Though I would go through the motions and use my creativity in this program, my treatment would not 'take hold' or 'stick' because I was only there because I had to be. I wanted to be able to be "healed" by this program, but the program simply wasn't striking me as being in touch with me enough to have the impact that it should, so that the desire for the drink or to drug would cease to exist. Nothing helped me forget my troubles or feel better like having drinks and using drugs. NA was a program that you had to "work" if you wanted it to work for you. I didn't get it. I was beginning to see how talking about your addiction and getting some feedback helped me to feel better, but I still wanted to use. What was I not getting or was this thing for real?

When I was at my first treatment center a few years back, we had group sessions that were similar to NA groups. The difference was that my counselors in that treatment center also had psychiatrists who went back and tried to understand what happened to you in the first place to make you want to use. NA focused on what you were dealing with now, what you had to say about your experiences, and steps you needed to complete to move on and not drink and use drugs. Weren't we skipping the cause at its root this way? Was I and everybody else in the program being set up to fail?

We had to learn the philosophy behind the center verbatim and interpret it before we completed our program as well as complete the group sessions and assigned projects as we moved forward in the program. It didn't help that one of the counselors went MIA and we later discovered that she was using again. It bothered us because this particular counselor was well-liked and a favorite of many because she knew our experiences from personal experience all too well, and could speak to us from the "other side": She had been there and knew how to stay in recovery.

I always thought that discussing what we did when we used and discussing how we used could create a trigger to use. Who was to say that a trigger was not "pulled" in her by her listening to us? As we had our moment of silence for her, I felt like the whole focus was off in that program.

We could smoke cigarettes outside in the smoke area in the back of the building so I smoked when I was out, because when I came back in after work, it was after hours for the smoke area and it was closed.

There was shopping a couple of days a week and we could go shopping as a group only. We had to sign out and we had a predetermined time to be back and sign in. I worked weekends, so I was there only sometimes to shop. Other than that I just worked and attended my required meetings and assignments. And I paid my required work release fees.

When I had completed the program, I moved back to the section of Richmond, referred to as Church Hill, in Richmond City's East End. While I was there I was a crime victim of a guy that used to deliver furniture from a rent-to-own place I bought from. He had always seemed perfectly harmless and I didn't think anything of him offering me a ride to get me some cigarettes late one evening after the stores closed. I had been walking back to the house after not being able to buy any. He gave me a ride to the store and we were supposed to be going back to the house where I lived with Uncle Joe, an adopted uncle of mine.

He had other plans for me and began getting on the highway. I asked him where we were going and he didn't answer me. I was starting to get a nervous feeling in my stomach. He had gotten Kools instead of Newports and now he was taking me somewhere. He pulled in between two warehouse buildings and drove to the rear of the lot and told me, with a gun to strip. I asked him if he was going to kill me too, and he said "I don't know." He began to take me and I didn't offer any resistance because I was scared that he would blow my head off. Suddenly he stopped and proceeded to find a corner to piss in and when he turned his back, I took off running through the woods.

I could hear him in the distance calling me. I even heard him say he was not going to hurt me. "Yeah, right," I thought to myself as I kept running as fast as I could. I ended up at a glass door on the side of a building about 3 blocks away from where Kevin stopped and I was and there was a camera there. I waved frantically at the camera and banged on the door again and again and no one came. So I found an open car and a jacket to cover myself. I didn't see anyone else anywhere. I saw a car riding by and ducked into the shadows beside the building because I was scared it was Kevin. I hid until I thought he was gone, and then I started walking toward the bridge I could see, and that is when I saw the police coming. By then it was dawn and I was finally safe.

The police took me directly to the hospital where they assigned me a police detective and the hospital performed a rape kit on me. At the time, I knew that if I gave my correct social security number that I would likely be arrested myself as I had not gone to see my probation officer because I had used before I went to see him the last time. So, I gave my daughter's social instead. They asked me if I had ever been to that hospital before, and I said no. To my knowledge, neither had my daughter ever been there. I was more concerned about going to jail than what had happened to me. I just wanted this behind me. It didn't kill me so I could move on. That is exactly what I wanted to do.

I would later be asked to identify my attacker, which I did at the hospital. The detective wanted me to testify against Kevin and I just wanted it to be over. He would never have that opportunity again and he didn't give me any disease. I just wanted to go. When the detective took me home, she told me she would want to talk to me in the next couple of days and a day or so later she called and told me to get dressed because she needed to get some information from me. I didn't want to go, but I didn't see how I could get out of it, so I got dressed and she came and got me.

Before we pulled off from the house, she told me that she knew that the social I gave the hospital was for my daughter. Apparently, my sister had taken my daughter to that hospital once when she was with her. Now she wanted my real social and when I gave it to her, she called it in, then she told me she had to take me in because I had a bench warrant. God might not forgive me if I told you the thoughts that ran through my mind in that moment, but I stayed cool and I just took the ride.

She was still talking and I didn't want to talk. I was glad she had some cigarettes and let me smoke all I wanted on the way. But I didn't really give a damn what she had to say right now. I guess I heard her and I didn't hear her. I think I answered her a couple of times in that daze I was in. I got out of the car and followed her into the jail from the holding area and just waited in that box looking out of a box-shaped window not as big as my face. I just waited for one of the trustees and a deputy to come and search me and give me a uniform and the basic necessities. Back in jail again. Damn!

I figured I may as well settle in. People I knew from being there before gathered around, asking why I was there since they never thought they would see me again. I didn't want to talk. I didn't want to tell everybody that I had just been brought in as a result of trying to help investigators with the guy who raped me. How was it okay to just bring me back to jail? I found out, when I discovered that she wanted me to testify against Kevin and she wanted me where she could pretty much depend on my being there. She promised that I would get out and into another residential treatment center before his trial. She asked me if I had used recently and I told her I had.

I just sat there and thought about the last few days. About how I got in the car with Kevin and what transpired afterward. I really didn't want it to go any further since I was okay. I gave a description of the car that was incorrect because I just wanted it to be over. I was really down because I wasn't working and Uncle Joe had to give me everything I got. I dated Uncle Joe's nephew Milton a few times and he smoked with me sometimes when he came over. I thought about where I was living and how I was living and how I should be able to do so much better. I felt ashamed that I couldn't seem to find any opportunity so I could hold my head up and go and get my kids. I called them because I felt so alone sometimes, even though it pained me when they asked me when I was coming to get them and I couldn't tell them anything. It seemed that my record eliminated me from worthwhile work.

So what was I going to do? I hadn't even thought about my book (yes, this book) in years and what had I learned that would answer some of the questions I had then? I already knew that until I could answer all of the questions and they all came together and made sense, that I had not finished learning. My children and my book kept me going in times like these when I wanted to give up. Things had to get better for me. There was no other way for things to go. But in the meantime, to get through to the next stages of my life, I knew I would use. What other way could I keep my sanity while fighting what seemed to be a losing battle? By using sometimes. That was "a given" just like it was "a given" that when I got high, I escaped into another reality where nothing mattered but the feeling I got, though short-lived. Other than getting that feeling that I got while getting high, I felt nothing because that was easier than feeling "less than" within my family and inadequate as a mother, because of my financial status (or lack thereof) and I felt pretty useless and insignificant--a nothing that with God's help would be something one day. That was my prayer--and my only hope.

Chapter 11

In five or six months, I was released to a residential treatment center in the downtown VCU area. Things went rather smoothly there. I wouldn't touch drugs only because I was tired of this unexpected ride and wanted to get off, even though I didn't have any idea what I was going to do with my freedom. I didn't know where to try next. I tried everything I could find when I got to Richmond. I looked everywhere. I only got the jobs nobody else wanted because they were the only employers who didn't care about my background. I would also be preparing to testify in court and had this meeting and that meeting with this office and that examining official. I didn't want to do it. I didn't want to testify against a sick black man and condemn him to jail for life. He needed therapy. What had gone wrong in his life? I mean what happened to make a seemingly normal and considerate person turn around in the darkness and become the kind of person who could violate women? If something happened (and something had to have happened), it broke him, and he could be fixed.

Shouldn't he be given one more chance, especially since I am okay? I think that somewhere I sensed his desperate anger at something other than me and I felt sorry for him, though I had the good sense to get away from him expeditiously. I saw his eyes angry then apologetic then angry, then sad as he overpowered me and I wondered what was going on in his head. Whatever his problem was, my instinct for survival kicked in and I wasn't going to stick around and be his next victim. But that didn't stop me from feeling sorry for him. I started out lying about the car's description because I wanted the whole thing to be over.

Since I got away I was fine, but I knew if I was picked up I could go to jail. Later I reasoned that I couldn't change my story now, so I stuck with the story, not really caring if they got him or not because I had to do time to be there to testify against him. I had already gotten away from this guy with my life. I resented that the detective deceived me and that I ended up locked up because she felt it was the best way to get me to court. Never mind that I had just been through a traumatic experience and that jail was probably the worst place for me then. I didn't trust her or the system. And I wondered what kind of person was I that I considered Kevin's feelings over my own.

The trial went on and I waited for them to call me to testify. Because of the car more than anything, I think, he was acquitted. I had found myself thinking that maybe I had put myself in that position because I was out late at night wandering around, and perhaps I deserved the scare of my life. And maybe he deserved another chance. After all, wasn't the system always locking Black men up whether they were guilty or not?

Hopefully he would recognize this as an opportunity to get his life together. I left the courtroom and returned to my program. Soon it would be time for me to leave that program and I would be working at a job I was told about by one of the men in treatment in the men's facility of the same treatment program. He was doing quite well there and it would have the best wage and benefits packages that I had the opportunity to get since I had been in Richmond.

I would be setting up appointments for salesmen (to present our company home exterior products) by going door to door and focusing on visible home improvement needs, convincing homeowners of the need for our products and a free estimate. I got a room at a boarding house on Parkwood Avenue in the Carytown area of Richmond, on the recommendation of the program director. She said that the owner was her brother-in-law.

Anyway, his name was Pete and the house was pretty clean, especially for a boarding house. My room was large with a dresser, bed and armoire. I immediately thought of my freedom from the program that was coming soon and of my friend JB with whom I had been conversing since I saw him, still looking good, at an NA meeting I went to one day. I hadn't seen him since college. He was one of a number of males I just had to have before I left the college.

It was perfect that he ended up living in the boarding house where I also rented a room in my junior year. Wow, it had been about 10 years since I had seen him. He was definitely looking forward to another encounter with me and he would be the one who would help me "break my room in". I ended up getting away because I had some free time one day, while I was still in the program. JB and I met in his room at the halfway house where he went after completing his program. We refreshed our memories about how it was to be with each other when we got together "back in the day" and we discovered that we had both learned a thing or two since then. Anyway, I moved on through the house for my tour.

The kitchen was upstairs, but the bathroom was right beside my room door. I remember thinking the rent was kind of steep, but it was a nice clean place to stay until could do better. I had to do better. I missed my kids and I needed to do better by them. I loved them and I missed them so much it hurt sometimes. All the things I always said I would do for my children and all that I would teach and show them, I had not done, and I was ashamed. The guilt was overwhelming sometimes and I would drink even though I was in recovery now. Drinking made me relax and feel better. I felt like I needed to drink, but had never been compelled to drink physically.

Even though I had a support system in recovery, there were things I just never shared. I didn't trust anybody. In fact, the last person I remembered trusting completely was my mother and I didn't trust anybody to take her place as confidant--she was my "go to" person for everything and no aunt, no sister, no friend would ever take her place. So, all of my most personal business stayed with me because there was no one I could trust as deeply as my mom. I could not show weakness to anyone, especially now.

I was in a new environment with all new people, except for JB who was going to be coming to my house in a few days. I needed that closeness of a man and I fully intended to enjoy him thoroughly, even if just for a little while. He was, after all, quite handsome and, though he didn't have a steady girl, I was sure he had to have someone in his life (not that I cared). Besides, we knew as recovering addicts that we should not enter into relationships for at least a year.

I had been in the room for a couple of months, when I learned that my cousin, Gregory was dead. It was such a shock. As kids, we had been very close. In fact, I was so much more like my mom's family-period. I slowly wrapped my mind around the fact that he was gone. I had lost my cousin Bobby as well, and I just wondered what the world was coming to.

I went to the funeral with my sisters and enjoyed seeing most of my mother's family. My Uncle Burl and Uncle George were looking at me, I noticed, and I asked them why they were looking at me like that. They said, "you are just like your mother, even your mannerisms and movements". I had been told that more than once and I remembered that I vowed to my deceased mother a day or two before her funeral that as long as I lived, she would never die. So, I wondered how many of her mannerisms I had actually adapted as now being a part of me, without even realizing it. Now I was naturally me, so whatever movements or mannerisms I had now were my own, or had become my own. My mother is always in my heart, and I will never forget her, her ways, her heart, her looks, what she endured. I knew it was incumbent upon me to reach successes she had never reached, though she was one of the most intelligent women I had ever known.

When I returned to Richmond from the funeral it was business as usual. I continued to work and, for a time I went to regular meetings. I didn't know why I continued to feel so empty when I was alone. I knew no one in my neighborhood except my housemates and I really didn't know them.

My landlord lived in the living space on the other side of the bathroom but I didn't want to be friends with him. The girl who lived next door to me had just as large a room as I had and it looked like she had a whole apartment worth of furnishing in that room. It was full, but it was neatly stored. She and I had already struck up a friendship. She had a phone in her room and, in fact, she was the reason I was able to get the call about Greg. There was a couple and one other resident upstairs and we all got along and everybody cleaned up behind themselves and I was grateful for that.

JB and I continued to see each other, and I made sure I threw out my containers of alcohol and that there was no beer on my breath whenever he was coming by. The last time I saw him while staying there, I remember I had borrowed a book of bus tickets from a friend of Dee's and I had come home and waited for JB. We had "gotten busy" and then there was a knock on my door. When I answered it, it was Dee's friend and she blew up about my not having paid her yet and went on so badly about the $10 that JB thought it was a drug debt and got his clothes and got out before the argument was over.

It took me a month to convince him that there were no drugs involved. Not long after that, I was awakened by a light shining in my window and on my bed. I had Dee to call the police, but of course, no one was there when the police came. Then there was a guy named EW that my landlord knew and saw one day as he left my room. He told me he didn't want the guy there. I felt like I could have whoever I wanted over to visit as long as no illegal activity went on. Well Pete raised the roof the next time he saw him and gave me more grief and told me again, in no uncertain terms, adamantly that he never wanted to see him there again.

The next day I was speaking to an older gentleman, Mr. Louis C, whom I spoke to everyday on my way to work. He had a huge house on the next block and I told him about what happened. Turned out that he knew the same guy and he thought highly of him. Go figure. Anyway Mr. Louis C (the older gentleman) also mentioned to me that the entire upstairs of his house was vacant. He asked me what I was paying at Pete's house. When I told him, he offered me a lesser rent for a better setup and, like a flash, I moved down the block.

I knew that being at Mr. Louis C's would be a better move. First of all I was upstairs from Mr. C. I was also in a two bedroom apartment alone, though I was only responsible for paying the rent on a room. That was a deal no one would pass up. The only thing was that it allowed me a lot of idle time with no interruptions. That was good and bad: the privacy was great, but the loneliness was something that would prove not good at all. I had too much free time on my hands. With an addict, idle time is truly the devil's workshop.

I worked daily, not getting home until around 8:00 pm. When I got home, I was often tired as we did a lot of walking door-to-door every day. I began to have a beer every day. It wasn't long before I wanted to have a taste of coke. A couple hits wouldn't hurt. Smoking coke was always my best kept secret. Who would know? Before I knew it, I had talked myself into it. I kept my use under control for a while, but eventually, I was having a beer and a hit every day. Mr. C was beginning to comment on my walking the floors at night, which was a sure sign that paranoia was setting in. You see, everyone who smokes crack has his own trip. Mine was putting everything up like my "hitter" and any loose coke. What would happen is that I would take a hit and have the euphoria, which would be immediately followed by an uncontrollable urge to put all paraphernalia out of sight, before someone could come in and catch me getting high. Never felt that urgency until after I had a hit, then suddenly I had to put everything away. I would also imagine that I heard someone in the apartment, so I would walk around to make sure no one was there. That is the walking Mr. C. heard.

He figured out what was going on after a while and confronted me about it. I had been in an accident while at work going from one location to the next. I hit my head on the windshield. I wasn't badly hurt. I had some pain and the doctors were concerned and ran multiple tests. I had to go to physical therapy and get heat packs and I had a prescription for a form of Percocet which I sold for $100, and instead I used the 800 mg ibuprofen to treat my pain. Anyway, with the time off, I was also getting high during the day. That's when he confronted me. He told me how disappointed he was and told me he expected it to stop.

I was expecting workmen's compensation and would not be able to pay him until the money came. But when the money came, I spent some getting high and wanted to give him half the check, which he would not accept. He told me instead that he expected me to move within a couple weeks. There I went again losing something else.

From there I ended up at another user's house (Donald) who listened intently to my plight while we used. Then told me I could stay with him, which I did. I realized that my addiction had become worse: it had picked up where it left off. I began to realize that my use was controlling everything in my life. I did everything around my next hit. I planned what I would pay before I got my check and made sure I raced to pay what I was going to pay before I took hit because I would blow my money getting high and be sitting around looking stupid with nothing. I would only ask my family for money I really needed and I would do what I said I was going to do with it, most of the time.

My conscience was not dead, though I was quite sick. Sick enough to do whatever I had to do in order to get my drugs. That included sexual favors for the men I dealt with like Donald, who always had a steady flow of money to buy drugs. I was not interested in Donald as a man and thought he was quite ugly, but it was a place to stay. And I couldn't let my family know that I lost my job, because after the accident I was confined to the office phones. I was not as good on the phone making appointments as I was in person, door-to-door, so my numbers went down and I was fired.

It wasn't all bad with Donald. His conscience and soul was not dead either because of the drugs. It was he who convinced me to go to church with him and it was at that church that my understanding of the Christian faith would be increased to the point that it would override what I had learned in Islam, returning me to the faith of my fathers, or the Christian faith. At that point in my life, the only church I had attended regularly before was the Baptist Church in the country where I lived my adolescent years.

When I would go to Sunday school, I would ask questions like "Why do we have to pray to God through Jesus?" I was told that I was being blasphemous to ask the questions that I asked, so I stopped asking them. I believed enough, when the invitation was extended at revival by a guest preacher, to accept Christ and be baptized, but I knew I didn't fully understand. I thought that the elders who ran the Sunday school class were going to teach me. What I was concerned about at the time was whether or not my questions would ever be answered or if they should be answered. Would I understand in time or was I supposed to blindly accept all that I was told. Was that what faith was? Was it blind acceptance? What would happen if I lost faith because I didn't understand?

The first thing I learned when I went to church with Donald was that there was 'no condemnation to those who are in Christ Jesus, who walk not after the flesh but after the spirit'. Outstanding! I never knew that. Did that mean that no matter what I did in the past, if I turned my life over to God that I could no longer be condemned like I felt I was now? Then I learned what 'walking after the flesh' meant and 'what walking after the spirit' meant. I learned that walking after the flesh meant 'walking' (living life) with the most important things in your life being physical and material to satisfy the physical body: That 'walking after the spirit' meant walking after those things in life that were spiritual.

Just that one bit of understanding of that concept of God's word had relieved me so much. I never knew it. It had never been explained to me before. In Islam you were expected to live life according to the principles set forth in the religion or you were considered not to be Muslim until you did. So in my years as a Muslim, I had considered myself to be 'non-Muslim' whenever, like now, I had not been living doing everything Muslims do, with the exception of making pilgrimage, which I couldn't afford to do yet. I couldn't wait to go to that church again so that I could continuously learn what I never could in the country church I belonged to before. Christianity was the faith of my forefathers, my direct descendants. Now was the time to see what truly was "natural" to me, as Islam was supposed to be my "natural" religion, according to what I had learned.

I remembered the time in the late 1970's that in my search for guidance to find the truth by direction of the Spirit of God, that the Spirit of God spoke to met, saying (though not in words) that I would recognize *The* truth because it would make common sense to me in every facet of physical and spiritual life: That each spiritual truth would be connected to the next, and would be connected to each reality of spiritual life and every science so that 360 degrees of understanding would be possible. While Islam did answer the questions about our condition as a people in this country, (which was the main reason I became a Muslim,) I had no peace in my spirit. My ability to rest in my religion of Islam was only possible inasmuch as I practiced the principles of Islam as the Islamic community thought I should. That meant that Islam was conditional. Would I discover that Christianity was an unconditional religion? I couldn't wait to find out.

Chapter 12

Donald and I continued to go to church and I learned more and more information that I never knew before. Each time we went I grew stronger and my understanding increased. Before we decided to go to church regularly, we recognized that what we were doing was really crazy. I would never be reunited with my children or have any success until we stopped. I began to love Jesus like I never had before because the Holy Bible was now becoming real in my life and not just a bunch of stories telling what people did wrong and how God punished them. And love God and Jesus you had better do, or you will die eternally. That was all I had ever gotten from Christianity before. Christianity and Islam before now had seemed like "do-it-or-die" religions. It seemed like God was threatening us all, and that was why we went to churches or temples.

With what I was learning, there was a now a reason to embrace Christianity, to want to be in church. I had so much to learn and I had heard so many things in church that now began to make sense. The more I learned, the less I wanted to use. I was excited in a way that I had never been before. My soul was alive. It was a blessing to go to church and I felt fortunate that I was going with someone who knew my plight with drugs and understood the struggle.

Everything went so well for months and I was learning so much that I never knew. Why had I not heard the things I was learning in all of the years I went to church? Why was it only here that I began to understand? Was the Baptist church in Virginia just that far behind in knowledge back then? I had never heard that "no weapon formed against me will prosper", that if I "believed in the Lord, that he died for my sins and was raised from the dead, I would be saved", or that "faith cometh by hearing and hearing by the Word of God". If I had heard such things before, I certainly did not hear them with understanding. When I went to church, it seemed that the preacher was always pointing out human shortcomings and telling us how God's wrath would come upon us if we didn't change our ways. There was no feeling of uplift, nor was there any edification. There was no "being translated into the Kingdom of God for us, only for the disciples.

In fact, the more I thought about it, my understanding of Biblical teachings back then was that the prophecies of the Bible referred to Jews and disciples. That was a fault of the old Christian Church in rural Virginia. Wherever I went, it seemed, in that rural Virginia town, I got the same message: "Do what the Bible says or die." Perhaps that was why many of us did not like going to church. I didn't know.

It had been perhaps 15 years since I had attended the Baptist Church. Perhaps the growth that caused me to now begin to understand the Christian faith had happened during those years that I did not go to church, and now the entire Christian faith was alive and teaching a living Word, that I now received. I knew that was true to a certain extent. In fact, I remembered the Pastor of the church in Virginia, Reverend Pryor and I remembered that he often cried each Sunday. I don't remember which family member told me, though I believe it was my mother, but what was said was that Reverend Pryor cried because he did not know if what he was telling us in the pulpit was true. He had his doubts, so was it any wonder that I had had mine?

I actually remember asking "Why do we have to pray to God through Jesus", just because of my curiosity. The answer I got from

143

my Sunday school teacher was that I shouldn't question God. That it was blasphemous to question what He had told us to do. Clearly, that elder did not know the answer to the question, which I would learn much later, had a simple answer. But if someone could live to be 60 years old and not understand the answer to that question, as a Christian, how could I ever get the answer?

Surely the Christian church had grown in knowledge and understanding and I wondered if it had anything to do with the knowledge Muslims had. Did Islam cause the Christian church to study its principles and really understand what it was that Christians believed, since Muslims knew so well what they believed? Was it because some Pastors were learned and some were not. Is that why I could now understand what the Christian church was teaching? I believed it to be so.

I knew that at one time, a minister didn't have to go to school to be a Christian minister, all he needed was a following to start a church. I hoped seminary school was now required for Christian ministers so they couldn't just get up in the pulpit and just tell the congregation whatever they thought inside their minds. I learned that was called "leaning on one's own understanding" and God said not to do that.

Chapter 13

It wasn't long before Donald began to slip into his old self. One day I returned to the house and found him wanting to have sex. We had said that we would not be getting high and that we would study the Bible each night to keep us in line and on the right path, and not have sex. He would sleep on the couch and I in his bedroom. We would even smoke cigarettes outside. Now he wanted to have sex. I took that to mean that he had been smoking crack while I wasn't there. I was disappointed. I wanted to hold on to what I had found spiritually and I knew that if he got high around me that I would soon join him. I wasn't there yet where I could be around crack and not smoke it, even though I was growing closer to God.

I had hoped Donald would deny using because then he would hide it from me if he got high. As luck would have it, he didn't and, of course, I ended up indulging. But I had just gotten a position as a teacher's assistant and I realized that I would have to move on. I did not want that lifestyle for myself any more. I would be training all summer for the position and I needed to go. We went to church that Sunday and while we were there, Donald picked at me. He started saying that I thought I was better than him and that he was going to tell the church that I had gotten high again. He just wouldn't leave me alone, and continuously said what he would do against me because I was growing closer to God.

Previously, he had told me that his family was cursed and now I was starting to believe it. First of all, he would look just like a demon if he had pointed ears. He had large lips and his scalp had deep creases and indentations all over it. This church believed that speaking in tongues was an ability that we all had. On the day that I accepted Christ back into my life and was taken back to the area where we all went to be presented to the church, we said a prayer that asked the Holy Spirit to give utterance to our unknown tongue that would be our personal language to God and we learned to just let that flow. Even from the very first day that I heard Donald speak in his unknown tongue, his voice sounded unfamiliar and unlike him-- To me, it sounded demonic. He had told me also that his sister could not even go to church because the minute she did, a demon or spirit began to touch her sexually to the point that she would always have to leave the congregation for the bathroom. I told Donald that if he didn't shut up and leave me alone, that I would get up and move from where he was so that I could hear the message. He finally quieted down. On our way back home in the church van, I decided I had to go from his house. Even though he had been responsible for my return to the fold by taking me to a church that taught me, I could not loose what I had now gained and I sought another place to stay.

I ended up calling my cousin Bruce who had visited me once while I was living at Mr. C's. He had a problem with crack and was working on his problem. At least if I went to his house, I wouldn't have the added pressure of a man who was interested in me sexually, wanting me to perform sexual favors for him while he was high or getting high. My cousin and I could help each other. But Bruce was still in active addiction and I soon found that I was using again as well. What was lacking in what I had learned, such that couldn't seem to get through to this compulsion I had to get high? Was something missing? At first just the knowledge of Jesus and our relationship to Him as joint heirs in the Father's kingdom was such a wonderful revelation that it sustained me. Now I was using and felt really badly afterwards. Well, I didn't have the pressure of a man trying to get with me sexually right after I hit. Maybe that's why I got high again: because I wouldn't have sexual pressure and could be high in peace. But more likely, I needed to know more. I needed more change in my spirit. A change in my spirit would change everything, I thought. And I did learn more. I learned that change was possible and that I did not have to stay in the state I was in. I would gain strength with each new thing I learned.

Donald came to Bruce's house and begged me to come back to his house. He said he couldn't stay clean without me. Little did he know, I was starting to get high again. I had been offered a job at the academy behind the church, which the church owned. I was in training for the summer and I would be a teacher's assistant. I only got high a few times, and I would stop that. I was determined to do well in my position under the umbrella of the church. I was determined that I was going to change my life.

Since I was still getting high over my cousin's house, and I decided I needed to get closer to the church. I spoke to the administrators at the church because I knew that the church owned property surrounding the church and that some of it was rental. The church had no vacancies, but there were other buildings near the church that had vacancies. I spoke to the church about a room a block away. The church would help me financially to get into one of those rooming houses and purchase a refrigerator that I would use as long as I was there. So I was all set.

But it wouldn't be long before I would realize that the building wasn't the safe haven that I thought it was. People were selling drugs, albeit covertly. I knew. I could see the transactions even as discreetly as they were made. Was there anywhere that drugs were not running the show? Not anywhere I had been. That is except for at home with my family. They were clean and drug free (of street pharmaceuticals). I know that this crack had come out of nowhere and had become an epidemic overnight. I remembered the first time I tried it. It left you with a compulsion to just keep doing it over and over again and I was unable to stop. Rashad had learned about the drug and had started doing it in the daytime while I was at work. Then I started a bit later. Next thing I knew I was in full blown addiction.

It was like nothing I had ever experienced before and the worst part about it was that it was the only drug I had ever taken that made me lose control. When I first started using with Rashad, it was like I couldn't stop. The crack was potent and plentiful. What I used to get in a vial for $10 would likely cost $40-$50 now, and the addiction was no less severe though the crack wasn't nearly as strong unless I really got hooked up with someone who had a good batch. It would be years before I realized that I was only hooking up with guys who got high as well. That way I knew I would never be judged by my man.

My life was a mess. When Bruce had stayed at my house, I wasn't getting high on crack. I was drinking and smoking weed. In fact, I almost put Bruce out when I discovered him smoking in his room because I was trying to stay away from hard drugs. I had actually quit using crack and just stuck to drinking beer and smoking weed. But by the time he left, I was using. I blamed Bruce and Robert for getting me started again and I blamed Rashad for getting me started in the first place. But nobody had put a gun to my head.

Seeking refuge, I contacted an old friend in the Churchill area not far from the apartment I had at Fairfield Court Projects. He rented or owned the same home for many years and he wanted me to move in before, but I didn't go because I knew that even though he was probably 60 years old, he had a romantic interest in me. I was not attracted to him in that way, and I knew that because he was older and so obese that he wouldn't give me many problems in the sexual department, and he didn't want me to pay any bills, but to just take care of my own financial needs. Clearly it was a better arrangement. In a flash, I left and returned later to get my things. Now I could settle into my job at the school and continue to grow in the Lord because right now I didn't have a chance. This would be my opportunity to get back on track because James F. only drank and I could handle being around alcohol.

I had been living at James' for about a month and a half. The school year had started and I went to church each Sunday and was beginning to grow even more in the Lord. I had learned to confess my sins to the Lord and to "turn things over to Him". I learned that by "Jesus' stripes I was healed". I learned to pray to God the Father "in the spirit" or in my unknown spiritual tongue for periods of time per day. I learned that blessings would come from the Father just for praying in the spirit. I learned to read the Word daily so that the Lord could "sow it in my heart" as I came to understand it.

I was grateful that the Lord had moved in my life and brought me out of darkness, returning me to the light of His Word. I loved my job because I was in the presence of the saints of God daily. I was learning to walk closer and closer to God. All was well with the job and I was given more and more responsibilities as a teachers' aide for the two advanced Pre-K classrooms. Not only did I prep for classroom instruction, but now I worked with the children who were having challenges keeping up in the classroom. I additionally had the huge aftercare group to hold from class dismissal at three until 6:00pm, when I completed my workday. I had the children to do a daily devotion which included standard prayer and confessions, which the children learned to lead and repeat independently. There was also always an activity or two for the children to participate in after a recess period and snack. We generally ended the day with a movie, most often a religious one. I was comfortable in my job and I loved working there.

I had run into a guy named Kenny that I knew on a Saturday while I was at a store down the street from James' house. I always thought he was attractive. He was missing one of his eyes and wore a patch over it. He was slimmer than I remembered.

We caught up with one another about what we had done and what we were doing with ourselves since we had last seen each other. He let me know that his father had passed and that he was now at his father's house alone. We had always made eyes at each other when we saw one another in the past and he invited me over for dinner. I decided to talk it over with James, who knew I would have other men in my life anyway because he could not keep up with a woman my age. Still, I wanted to respect him by telling him what was going on. I felt better that he knew what was going on and Kenny only lived a block or two away. That night we had dinner and drinks. We were also intimate. The sex was the best I had ever had. I came to discover that his secret was that he had snorted some heroin. I took a couple of toots but that wasn't my thing because it made me nauseous, so I drank and smoked some weed instead. Little did I know that tonight would lead to a relationship. Weeks later, I would move out of James' house and into Kenny's house, assuring James that I would keep in touch and visit him. James thought it was a big mistake, but I was hell bent on going, so he conceded.

I was at Kenny's only for about two months when the relationship became violent. I had already discovered that Kenny smoked crack as well before I moved in. We started out indulging only on weekends and that use was minimal, just to boost the sexual experience with him (boosting him, not me). But, of course, the use began to spill over into week day use. I was adamant that I loved my job and was not going to endanger my position.

For almost a year, I maintained that position without any incident. But as time wore on, the abuse and the fact that I was "living in sin" or in a sinful relationship started to pull at my conscience and I was convicted by my beliefs as being wrong to have this relationship. But Kenny had control. He controlled everything. When I got paid in the past couple of weeks, we had started to use the majority of my check to purchase crack, cigarettes and beer. All of my money wouldn't go in one night but I was broke within days. I had to be sure to purchase bus tickets, toiletries, and food items on my lunch break before I went home. If I didn't do it that way, I wouldn't have what I needed for the next two weeks because everything was closed when I got off. Kenny always met me at the bus stop, so I could not be late catching the bus or would be accused of messing around with another man, which was an automatic argument if not an outright physical confrontation.

I had experienced that with him before and didn't want to be the cause of the next argument. Of course, in time I would mess up and not get everything on lunch break like I should, so I would run short of what I needed. So I would begin to take bus fare from the coffee fund by the coffee pot at work. There was a time that i would take from fundraisers and field trips that the church trusted me to collect during the afterschool hours. My conscience was tearing my ass up. And the Academy administrators were beginning to miss the money. I wanted to stop, but Richmond bus drivers were not taking any excuses only money and bus tickets. I had to get home. But every time I took something I felt so very bad and was so ashamed and guilty that I was sure people could see it all over my face. I would get to work knowing I had no money to get home and knowing I had to find a way to get home. I was always preoccupied with the knowledge that I had to work something out by the end of the day so I could get home, and sometimes so I could get high.

On a few occasions, the dean had met with me wondering what was going on with me and asked if there was anything I needed to discuss with her. She said they were accustomed to checking with all the new teachers to be sure they were adjusting to their environment at the school. I could hardly look at her but forced myself to do so. I put on a confident smile and went back to work. It wasn't very long before they would figure that I could be connected to the missing money. When I was called to the office to see what I knew about the missing money, I wanted to cry out, but I was afraid. If I told them it was me taking money, they might fire me. Kenny would really be mad because of the loss of income. I wasn't thinking about the fact that the Church might help me, I just hid behind a mask so ashamed I didn't know what to do. You would think they would have fired me then, but they didn't.

Then there was the incident in the afterschool program when I thought I heard a child use the F word and other children reacted as though that was what he said. When the child's father came, I told him that the child used the F word and immediately he took his son into the bathroom and was going to discipline him. I struggled with whether or not to say I was not absolutely sure, but said nothing. Moments later the father came back out and said that his son denied saying the F word. It was then that I told him that I thought that was what I heard as well, but was not absolutely sure. There was a meeting the next day and I was no longer head of the afterschool program, but I still had my job. The incident that ended the job was when the little VCR was taken and the school believed I did it. The day it went missing, I had a lot of gifts so it was either Valentine's day or Christmas, when parents tended to bring gifts for teachers.

I did take it and when I got home with it, Kenny said "I can't believe you did this, you love that job." But I was concerned about not having any money when I got home and hoped to sell it, so that we could get high. The next day when I got to my main classroom, the children were watching the tv with another VCR so I thought all was well.

Before naptime I was called to the office and questioned. The end result of that meeting was that I was fired. The dean of the school had me to sit in her office. She asked me about the missing VCR and of course I denied knowing anything about it. She said she wished she could prove all of the allegations against me, but could not. I sank deeper and deeper into my seat it seemed as she talked. When she finished she asked me if I had anything to say. When I didn't really say anything, she showed me she had more of an insight to what was going on with me than I thought. She said that she wasn't sure what was going on but had felt in her spirit that I was going through something and needed help but that I had tied their hands by not sharing what was going on. She said that the person and the spirit that was therein me when I got to the academy had seemed to change and she hoped I got it together and completely returned to God. Then she handed me my check and said I could go now.

I was so heartbroken and ashamed as I walked to the classroom and gathered my things and left the school. She was right and I didn't know what to do with myself. As I rode home on the bus, I sank into a depression mixed with disappointment in myself. I didn't know how I would tell Kenny, but I would drown out my depression in alcohol and drugs. I knew I would because that was all I knew to do. I didn't feel good unless I used, especially after something like this. I had destroyed my life and I didn't know if God would ever forgive me, but I asked him to.

What was I missing and why couldn't I let drugs go, I wondered. Would I ever reach the mark? Why in the midst of all that I was learning was I still using. Was it just stubborn resistance or was there something else that I didn't realize that I needed to do. Why didn't God deliver me from my usage? I felt trapped in a life of drug use and the abuse of a man that I had tried to please. Whenever I stole money and even when I stole the VCR, I was doing it so that I wouldn't go home empty handed and so I could provide for our getting high that day. I did it so Kenny would go out when I got home and forget for a while to argue and we could have a peaceful night. How would I ever tell my family?

My younger sister had come to the Church on two occasions: once over the summer as we trained and once while I was conducting the afterschool program. She was impressed and I was so glad she had come. The Spirit of God was in the school and the Church so strongly you could almost tangibly feel it. But I couldn't be in the Church 24 hours a day, and when I left, the old feelings and old habits came back. I didn't know what I was missing but I had to find it to stop using. But not today. Today I planned to be very high and very intoxicated rather than to feel what I was feeling right now.

Chapter 14 (1998)

Life went on with Kenny. I was hardly ever allowed to leave the house alone. When I first began living with him, I had snuck out of the house to go and get us some drugs while he was asleep. My clothes were wet because I got caught in the rain. I couldn't find anything and just returned to the house, leaving my clothes downstairs in the hall. I just returned to bed and went to sleep.

In the morning Kenny decided to go out, and when he went for the door, he discovered I had been out because I had left the top lock off. That was the beginning of the end of his trusting me and it was downhill from there. I continuously tried to fix it by giving all that I could and by trying to please him in every way that I could, but ultimately it was never enough. He would never trust me and he restricted my movement now that I had no job.

Regular money stopped coming into the house. The water got turned off. We were reduced to getting drinking water from the lady next door and the bathing, cooking, cleaning and flushing water we got from catching rainwater in barrels outside. Kenny worked almost daily for some drug dealers who lived about 5 blocks away.

He did odd jobs for them and they paid him in drugs mostly. I often wondered if that was what he had been doing all along but I dared not ask. Anyway I began to use more. He didn't hold on to any money for me to search for work, so I would call my family and ask for money to help with household bills and transportation to get around. I always paid the bills but I sometimes didn't look for work. That is, if Kenny said he wanted me to stay at home or that I couldn't go. When company came, I stayed in the bedroom we shared until he came and got me or until the company left.

Kenny was working on a disability claim and his sister had come back to live with us. She also smoked crack and they often didn't see eye to eye and argued a lot. After a time, she left and didn't come back. Kenny's disability came through and he got a substantial check. With it he did everything but turn the water back on. He bought a keyboard, a truck, satellite TV and all the drugs we could smoke. He invited others over that he knew, all female, of course.

By the time that money ran out, another check was on the way which he also frivolously spent. At least he let me get my hair done by buying the perm. He kept telling me that the truck was for me but how was I supposed to get insurance, license plates, registration for the vehicle and I wouldn't be driving without it. It was a way to escape, but I could never get away unless the car was straight, having all legal documentation. So I just got high and ate when I wasn't high. I just existed. Kenny often degraded me and made me feel worthless, which fed my depression and kept me getting high. My brothers had come to visit me a couple of weeks earlier. I thanked God it wasn't cold because I didn't want them to come into the house. I was ashamed of where I lived, especially with no running water. But my youngest brotherDouglas wanted to use the bathroom and I reluctantly allowed him to use it. I kind of figured that he would leave a few dollars in the medicine cabinet and I would hide it from Kenny.

My eldest and closest brother, Eric needed me to come home so that I could care for his home because he had surgery coming up. I didn't give him an answer yet but I would soon. I knew that Kenny would never let me go. But I wanted to go. I decided that the next time I was abused (which was regularly), I would leave. I would call my brothers and go.

So the very next night that we fought, I escaped to a pay phone and called my brother and told him to come get me because I couldn't take it anymore. The next day, even though Kenny had talked me into staying, my brothers and my uncle came and we packed my things into the vehicle and left.

Now I was back into the fold of my father's side of the family and I would live at my brother's house which was across the road from my aunt's house where my children lived. I had been beaten and didn't want the children to see me that way, so it took me a couple of days to go over and see them. I had asked my aunt to give me time to get it together before sending them over.

Of course my children wanted to know when we would be moving in together once they saw me and I told them I was working on it. And I did work on it. When I had been at the Church in Richmond, I had learned that the Lord would "open up the windows and pour me out a blessing that I would not have room to receive" if I tithed. So even though I screwed up in a major way and lost my job (and a great deal of self-respect) I did tithe while I was still working. For one thing, I felt that the Church would know if I did not tithe, but I was also hopeful that the Lord would see fit to deliver me from drug use because I tithed. I was only able to tithe because I cashed my check on lunch break and tithed before I returned to work. If I waited until Sunday, I wouldn't have the money to tithe. Also I wasn't going to Church regularly in those last few months before I was fired.

I prayed for my own place and that God would provide the means to move. In the meantime, I went over to my aunt's house across the road daily to visit my children and talk about what my plans were and we talked about the fact that I needed to stay with my brother for a while to care for his two minor children while he recovered. My brother went into surgery and came home after some time in the hospital. He was on all sorts of medication. He kept spiking a fever and ended up going back into the hospital with infection in his scull bone, which had to be removed and treated. But he did recover to the degree that he became self-sufficient again.

It would be months before I would feel comfortable leaving. By the time I was comfortable about leaving, I had a job. I had been attending church regularly since I had been home and felt like I was back on track and ready to have my own place and my own classroom. I searched for a place and then out of the blue my aunt's cousin called and said she needed someone to live in her mother's house because the person currently living there was moving. It was an old, but well-kept house. There were 5 bedrooms in the house and there was an upstairs and downstairs. God truly had poured out a blessing to me that day. All I had to do was pay the utilities. During my search I had become frustrated, but I kept the faith and I truly believed that God had another place for me since none of the ones I applied for came through. I kept telling people when I was turned down that "God has something else for me". Sure enough, He did.

I just couldn't stop praising Him that day. The icing on the cake was that I was also going to be getting my own car, which is essential in the "country". My little sister, Maureen was getting a new car and I could pay off her old one in a few payments, so that was what I did. My children and I finally moved into the house once the lady who was there moved out. At last we were a family again and had our own house with more than enough space for us. I chose my bedroom first, then let the children have their pick of the remaining bedrooms. I was on top of the world and I had God on my side. He was hearing me and had answered all of my prayers. I couldn't have been more grateful.

All was well and I settled into a job teaching at a local preschool headed by my new Church. I already knew my employers as friends of my family as well as brothers and sisters in Christ. The Church was very spirited and I realized that the Church in Richmond was Pentecostal in its nature as well as my new church. I needed to know more about God and I wanted to discover those things that I did not know by regular attendance. Turned out that the things I knew had already had begun a transformation in me. But that transformation was far from over. I knew that everything began with faith.

I had trusted God and believed in his ability to intercede on my behalf in all phases of my life and my faith, not in the workings of man but in the workings of God. He was why I had the home I now had. When there seemed to be no hope in my finding somewhere for me and my children that I could afford, God had control and caused my distant elder cousin to contact my aunt, who let me know that I could stay at her deceased mother's home. It was true that God would "open me the windows of Heavens and pour me out a blessing that I would not have room enough to receive" because I tithed and was faithful to His Word.

The children and I really enjoyed the home and all had our areas that we enjoyed most--mostly our bedrooms. Dorian liked his room but stayed in the adjoining room with his games. And Sheba, the girly girl that she was, liked being in her room doing girly things like trying on different outfits, experimenting with hairstyles, etc. I was either in the kitchen or in my room on the phone or watching TV. We enjoyed our privacy and the children loved the fact that they didn't have to deal with the outside preferences or household rules of other family members. All they had to deal with was me and my rules and expectations. It simplified things for them and everything was coming from Mom, and I intended to mold them into productive, respectable members of society. I was glad my children both still had several years left in school, which would give me time to be their guide and reestablish myself in their lives as their mother and nurturer.

My aunt had done this for several years. I was so grateful to her and my uncle. Had it not been for them, I don't know what I would have done. I was an addict and I took years to get the learning about addiction that would enable me to stick to any recovery program. Now that I was here "in the country" I could be abstinent and put distance and time between use and actually stay in recovery.

Staying in fellowship with God would be the best way to make abstinence work for me. There would be no meetings because none were available. I also had no car and you couldn't even go to the closest store without one. So I could also not get to any drugs because I knew no one who had them and I had no car to get to them if I did. I joined the Church of God in Christ that I attended. I remembered the Baptist Church I had attended while still a child, when we moved to Virginia from Washington, DC. I was an adolescent at the time. I didn't get answers to my questions. At the Church of God in Christ, I got answers. At the Church in Richmond, I got answers. Neither of those churches was the Baptist church and I wondered if the Baptist church even held the necessary knowledge to lead one to God, and not lead you to join just because joining the church was what one was supposed to do at a certain age.

So when I returned to Buckingham, I didn't even go to my former Baptist church which I joined at the age of 12 or 13. I went to the Church of God in Christ, and I joined. I knew the people who were at the head of the Church. They were my employers as well as they had become like family; they attended family gatherings and were treated as family. My little sister was already a member and quite active in the Church when I got back.

I began to teach the adolescents at the Church and I continued to flower in my knowledge and understanding of God's Word by receiving the message from the pulpit. I didn't want the Church to know that I had strayed away while in Richmond, and that I had returned to Buckingham in that state. I recomposed myself over a matter of a couple of weeks; my sister, Maureen permed hair and I began recovering from a wounded spirit, separated from the source of my pain. I continued to learn each Sunday to increase the knowledge of God and Christ that I already had. In the back of my mind, I could reestablish a renewed covenant with God and move forward without baring myself before them. I thought it might affect my job if they knew how I was before I came back. They might think I was unable to handle the responsibility of a class. One thing was for sure, I had enough information to be "sold" forever on Jesus, the Christ who had saved my soul by his sacrifice. I would learn and give and work in His service, so grateful for His bringing me back into the fold with my family. I was aware that I had a lot to learn about God, His Will and His Way still, I knew that.

Over the next several months I grew in the Lord tremendously. I was likely positively affected by the fact that my family was near me and I enjoyed it when my niece and nephew would come over and visit with my children.

They all went upstairs and I didn't hear from them until Maureen came to pick them up. They were like brothers and sisters. They had grown so close because they had spent several years together. My sister lived in Buckingham and was over at my aunt's house daily. My aunt was like a mom to her because she had raised her from a very young age. I used to take care of Maureen and watch out for her. I missed in my life for so many years. My parents only kept four of us for the entirety of our lives as minors. My two elder brothers were raised by my grandmother. But my siblings all knew who they were, even though they were raised by other family members, they knew who mom and dad were, as no one tried to take their identity from them. My elder brothers Eric and Alexis and Maureen would take on the values of my father's side of the family and the four of us would take on the values of my mother's side, because they also lived in D.C.

Mom used to say that my father's side of the family thought themselves better than her side. I learned that to be true when we moved to Virginia. My father's side chose favorites among children and they would support them and uphold them, right or wrong. My mother's side didn't choose favorites and just treated everyone the same way under the same value system. By the time my sister married (1986), my mother had passed away (1980), and my aunt and uncle stood in as mother and father of the bride.

Maureen and I had attended the same college. My grandmother had gone there when it was a trade school, and educated the senior population in Buckingham in a one-room school. My Aunt Elaine went there and was a retired teacher, then, Maureen and I went there. I went there after her, even though she was younger. When my mother had passed, apparently, my aunt thought it would be a good idea to offer me the chance to go to college. So I quit my government job and left DC to attend college.

While I was there I really studied hard. I was in the library when I wasn't in class because I wanted my evenings to myself. There was a party going on somewhere everyday even though it was a private, religious school. My first year on campus, I vowed to move off campus because I observed the polite and prim young ladies of my dorm acting like children all the time. They ran up and down the halls and made noise everywhere, but when they hit the lobby, it was a different story.

I was five years older than the freshmen who were at the Hall, and I had matured considerably. For the past five years, I had lived a semi-independent life. I lived with Teddy for a couple of those years and I just didn't play like that anymore. I felt out of place. Also I felt that I was too old to be told what time to come in, and how I should act and when I could go out, and what I could or couldn't do. But when I moved off campus, I think initially out of boredom, I became quite promiscuous. I had been faithful to Terry for the years we were together. Now I was a free agent. I knew he would be, so I was.

There were so many fine young men there, many of them quite athletic, and little to their knowledge I wanted them as much as they wanted me. I would play hard-to-get anyway, so I could get everything I wanted sexually, and would even purchase adult refreshments. I can say that I had my fill there. And to my shame, there was more than one time that I woke up not knowing where I was or how I got there. But I knew for sure that I had sex. Otherwise I wouldn't be there. I would be mad on those occasions because I blacked out and didn't remember anything because I drank too much. It was also a small town, so I didn't know who knew what happened that night. People talked too much about people in small towns and that was one of the reasons I didn't like them.

There was also Rashad whom I would end up marrying. I met him in my sophomore year. By my junior year, we were an item. He was quite athletic and very attentive. He wasn't the best looking guy in the world, but he wasn't ugly either. Once he hooked on to me, he never let go. He wouldn't go back to his dorm after he stayed over a couple of days. Sometimes I wanted him to go to his dorm and give me some alone time but it was like pulling teeth getting him to go.

Anyway, we were together so much that he grew on me. He was 5 years younger than me because he came to college right out of high school on an athletic scholarship. When I finished college in December 1985, he dropped out--right in the middle of the year. I had to retake a single course that was not offered in my final semester, so I finished in December, and would be returning in June 1986 to walk across the stage with my 3.0+ CGPA. By the time I walked across the stage I was working in the mortgage department of a bank and Rashad was a corrections officer. And we were pregnant finally after I had cried because I hadn't taken birth control for a year and some change, and I didn't seem able to get pregnant. My biological clock was running out and I wanted to have a baby before I was 30. I wasn't planning to have but one child. I just needed one before I got too old to have a healthy baby.

Little did I know that I would have one healthy baby and then another. He had yellow jaundice when he was born and we had to stay in hospital after he was born until it passed. He was another cesarean baby just like my first. Apparently my pelvic bones were too dense for my baby to pass through, for my first delivery (January 23rd 1987) and for my second, with all that happened with my first delivery, doctors did not want me to risk having this baby by natural child birth, and would induce my labor on (October 20th 1988). With my first baby, an epidural was injected into my blood stream instead of my spinal fluid and stopped my heart and I had to be revived and my baby taken by emergency cesarean section. The both of us could have lost our lives in my first delivery and my child was and is a miracle baby, and I a miracle mother. But the only thing good about this method of birth had to be that my vaginal wall stayed intact as it had not seen childbirth, only my womb had. But I had visible scars, especially when I had Dorian

We (children and I) enjoyed the house where we lived. Sometime after I had been back and had reestablished myself, I got a call from my cousin Bruce who was now about 20 miles away in a town known as Cumberland County, where he worked in the chicken houses for his paternal aunt, then for another farm. It was through him that I met the next man in my life, Harry.

Harry and I talked on the phone for at least an hour a day. He would call me in the evenings when he had a break from the chicken houses that were so huge that you could not see through to the opposite end of the isles. They hatched chicks and raised them a while, then shipped them off. We got to know each other asking about each other's lives and what our interests and plans were. Then the day came for us to meet. Bruce stayed with our Aunt Stella who had now moved back to" the country". At that time, she had not long ago returned to Buckingham where she grew up. It was her son, Gregory who had passed away and had left her some money and I guess she just decided she had had enough of the DC metropolitan area and wanted to be close to her roots. She was my favorite aunt, we were more like friends—Aunt Stella and I knew I would be at her house a lot.

On this particular day, I think it was the first day I had been to her house. Harry and Bruce were there. I liked what I saw when I saw him. He was tall and handsome and looked like the athlete he had been. I remember thinking that talking to him would be a waste of time, because he could not be interested in me. His type usually had a pinup girl for a girlfriend and I had put on some pounds since childbirth. So, I hardly looked at him, though we talked a lot. I was surprised to find myself still shy when I met someone I really liked and I shied away from him occasionally throughout the evening.

When we talked on the phone again, he told me he noticed that I kept him at a distance. He asked me why but I didn't answer him. Then he said, "you must think I am not the kind of guy to be interested in you or something." And I admitted that was true and he assured me he was pleased with what he saw and had more interest than ever. So we continued to talk and I ended up picking him up one night and bringing him to my house for a couple of days. That's when he passed the test. My companionship and sexual test, that is.

Over the next few months, we would become really attached to one another, dependent upon one another for companionship. Buckingham was a small town and one often learned to entertain oneself because the entertainment outside of the video stores was practically nonexistent. In fact, other than the video stores, there didn't seem to be much to do except church, unless, of course you went closer to Charlottesville or Richmond. There were also movie theatres, a bowling alley and restaurants in Farmville, which was closer. And no matter where you went, there was always shopping, even in Buckingham.

Harry and I would talk hours every day and my own children began to tease me about my "boyfriend". It wasn't long before Harry was staying with me. He had grown tired of tending chicken houses and the restriction of his movement because of the job. Chickens had to be checked on regularly as delicate systems within the houses had to be kept up. For example, they had to maintain at certain temperatures, they had to be cleaned, etc. All this work had to be done at the weirdest times of morning and night. Then fully grown the chickens had to be caught and put on a truck for slaughter or to lay eggs at other houses. He got a construction job pretty quickly. It was a new experience having a man to live with me. I had lived with Terry a couple years before and I lived with other men like Kenny, but this was the first time I had a man to live with me. I would have to determine what to charge him and balance that with our relationship. I had come to know Harry quite a bit from our conversations. According to him, he had been hurt before and we were on the same page: Neither of us could take the emotional pain of a person who cheated after making a commitment. Not to ever cheat was not a problem for either of us, because it just wasn't in our natures to cheat.

I knew that would be one thing that would continue to keep us together because it was truly hard to find a partner who could be trusted to be faithful, and especially one in whose nature it was to be faithful. I needed that (faithfulness) in my life.

Life with Harry was good for a while. We stuck close to home when we weren't working. I usually picked him up from work after I got off. It seemed to be working like a charm until the day that we scheduled that trip to Hampton Roads. We actually went because other family members were going there and it would be a good time to meet Harry's family, since he was from there as well. We packed clothes for a few days for each of us to wear. I had fried some chicken and we would stop on the road for other refreshments. I would have to keep the children away from so much sugar because they would have a difficult time being still for the ride, especially Dorian who had ADHD, which was improving. He was quite intelligent and often bored in class. I was glad that his attention deficit did not affect his learning ability, though it did sometimes cause problems in the classroom, as he could be disruptive because he wasn't listening or was doing something other than work. All in all, Dorian was a great kid, very loving and listened at home most of the time.

He had gotten his first play station for Christmas. And he knew his punishment for not listening or for being disobedient was losing his privilege to play the game. I was a great behavioral tool and simplified my job as a mother, I thought.

The family's cars and my car separated when we got close to Hampton Roads. The family was going to my sister's house and we were going to meet Harry's family. We first met his sister Raine where we left the children. Then we went to his cousin Jackie's house. Before we got there, Harry explained to me that his cousin was sick, but that she still got around and did whatever she wanted to do--including drugs. It was now that I learned that we would be spending time with friends of Harry's and going to the places he knew in his addiction.

We had brought a good amount of money with us. From what I could gather, we would be getting high. And so we did. After leaving Jackie's with promises to come back, we went to this crack house. It was a dingy, dirty little place. It was dirty not so much because it wasn't neat, but because the walls and the floors hadn't been cleaned in ages. Two sisters lived there along with anyone who wanted to flop there for a night or for a spell. An elderly woman whom they called Grandma lived downstairs in a room off the kitchen. No one ever saw her, but I had heard her during the day calling asking for food and water, which they would give to her. I thought this must have been her house at one time. No phone was there and I often wondered how it was that she was able to stand her living arrangements.

The sisters' bedrooms were where the people got high. Some in one room then some in the next. I was a little scared because this was the kind of house that people raided. Luckily we didn't stay there long either. Instead we went to the most dangerous place of all, a light blue colored house where drug dealers sold drugs. Harry knew them all, and when we went to this house we would get so high that I would go outside and turn the air on in the car. The higher I got, the more paranoid I became. But was this paranoia or common sense? The traffic was so heavy there at the blue house, it made me wonder why the police hadn't raided it long ago. Then I learned that they had raided it, but others set up shop again. I felt so out of place and I couldn't help feeling ashamed before God for what I was doing. I just knew God was saying "There you go again. Don't you have any strength at all? Any willpower in you?" That only added fuel to the fire: The worse I felt the more I used. It had always been that way since I could remember. The only time it had not been that way was when I was a minor.

I was so different, so strong then. I was a writer, able to put all sorts of emotions and feelings into words. I knew I was ashamed of my father and felt sorry for my mother in her apparent inability to leave my father and his abuse. I couldn't forget that day that Dad was on top of Mom restraining or fighting her and she told me to call the police, then my father said "if you do it, I'll kill you". I think something died in me that day because from that moment on I had a fear in the pit of my stomach because I was afraid of my father and now I knew he was capable of killing me. And if my father could kill me, was there anywhere in the world that I could be safe? Could I ever trust anyone? Family friends had molested me before and I think my father knew at least about PeeWee. I didn't feel like I could say anything because I wasn't supposed to like how it felt.

I was really messed up. And I continued to be messed up about my sexuality although I seemed to progress in other areas. I learned not to speak about things that happened to me sexually; not to say anything against a man in the family because to do so would be telling family business and I knew better than anyone not to say anything. And when we had moved from the city, there were times that I touched my friends as they slept because that was what happened to me, so I thought that was what I was supposed to do. But I have never been gay, and I'm glad I learned early that it was wrong when it happened to me and I shouldn't do it to anyone else, either.

Anyway I waited days on end for Harry to return and he did once every couple days. Then he would disappear again. I was scared to call my job or my family because i didn't know what was going on or when we would be able to leave. Whenever Harry was gone, I didn't know of a way to use the phone. Eventually, about a week later, we left. I called the family and my job and everybody let me have it. I just picked up the kids from my aunt's when i got back and set to getting another job since I was informed that I no longer had one.

I got the chance to move when I found my next job in a parochial school. I taught a first and second grade class most of the day, and an eighth and ninth grade English class for one period. I loved it. I just loved teaching children and giving them knowledge they never had. I looked forward to any challenges I would have because I would learn and grow too. Harry and I were still together but had made a pact not to get high anymore. The damage that trip had done would never be forgotten. I had learned during my life there that Virginia was a very unforgiving state and, naturally, so were most of its people. Not on the surface, but subconsciously.

Nobody seemed to think "outside of the box". When they did they learned to get back in their place. You stayed within the guidelines and did things the way they had always done them. You stuck out like a sore thumb if you didn't. And there tended to be a way to quiet those who came with new ways of doing things. Whatever "thing" they were talking about, they would stop talking about. The county did not embrace change, they were fine with things the way they were. I always felt I had better stay in my place. I never knew that one day I would look over my life and see that in spite of my fight to keep my individuality, my fight to keep them from breaking my spirit, that I would realize that they succeeded in breaking me and I no longer had confidence in myself or what I thought, and that what I saw, I saw through the eyes that I had been conditioned to view things through, as I adapted 'their way' as my way of thinking. It was the conditioning of incarceration: either you learned and did it their way or you never got out. The problem was that, once incarcerated, a person, especially a Black person, was as close to nothing as one could get. Everything around me reinforced the feeling. I was prone to hiding for the shame of what I had done. I no longer attended church. I wasn't worthy of God's love and grace. Nobody was, but I felt the unworthiness more than most.

I had to redeem myself. I knew I had to make myself look better in God's sight but i didn't know how to do it. I began to doubt my own reasoning and didn't value my own thoughts and opinions. I had been convinced that because I had gone to jail, I was the bottom of the barrel of people. Try to put your life back together when you're marked as a zero because you went to jail. All I had was the book that I began when I was in my twenties. I lacked the confidence I had back then, knowing I had a story to tell and a gift from God to tell it with. The need to tell the story was my driving force. It kept me going because I believed that it was inspired of God, but I knew I had more growing to do before I would be able to finish it. Back when I wanted to publish the first part of the book, I somehow knew in my spirit that the book would not be ready until I was near 50 or older because I could only write from the viewpoint of a young adult at the time of the completion of Part One. In order for me to have anything of great value to give to the world, I would have to know more from experience.

In the school where I was a teacher's assistant, I learned that "you can't teach what you don't know and you can't lead where you don't go." Surely I had to learn much that I didn't know in order to pass on any great truth to my readers. Time would tell, age and time would reveal more and more to me until my book was truly a work of art and a spiritual source to help others like me. I remember that my brother thought I should be less personal with some of the contents of the book. I also remember thinking that my book is to help the downtrodden and addicted, the hopeless and the cast out. I also felt that I could not help them unless I told the whole truth about my life, because only in doing so would my audience see me as themselves and identify on a deeply personal level.

With the help of God, I would come to know the words to walk myself and others out of the world that destroys their voices and mine. I knew that as a Christian, part of my duty was to bring others into the faith. I wondered why I was still prone to using drugs outside of the fact that I still had no real outlet that I trusted to speak to. Maybe that was a bigger deal than I made of it. I couldn't speak to teachers or the pastor where I worked about the problems I was having lest I bring my whole position into question, as to whether I could actually handle it. But I knew that having to hide what I was challenged with was unhealthy. I wished I could talk to my mother. After she died, there was not one person in the whole world I trusted completely.

I felt like I was by myself and that no one else would ever understand me, nor would they honestly care for me--all of me-like she did. People inside and outside of the family often twisted my words and tried to tell me what motives I had for doing things. That was because they came to know that I used drugs sometimes. I didn't want that life, yet I had still used. My family had help not trusting me through a family member who stayed on the phone and in their ears about me and her interpretation of who I was. I never took anything from my family because I felt they were all I had, even though I felt outcast now because of my use. I just did not feel like a part of them anymore, as they had all become successful. I was the only one struggling besides my brother, Eric, and now even he was doing well financially. And I knew that it was my own actions that caused me to feel that way. I didn't need someone in the family to encourage the family not to trust me and to make me appear worse than I really was. I think I may have some idea why she went out of her way to drive a wedge between me and my siblings, though: because I was outspoken and didn't feel like I had to do exactly what she or anyone else said to do with my life. Perhaps I didn't do things her way because I didn't trust her.

On more than one occasion she had been the confusion in our lives rather than the unity. I did love her, but I couldn't trust her. And she wasn't the only one in the family that I couldn't trust, she was the one who was the most vocal, who also either lied or put her twist on everything she knew (or half-knew).

My eldest brother was the only one who saw me as I was with imperfections, problems and needs. He helped me with his whole heart, and never asked that I do anything to deserve it. I think that if I had not had the financial woes over the years that I had, some resulting from my addiction, I would be more accepted. I was the only one of my siblings who had children, but no partner to lighten the load. Even if I didn't have a dependency problem, I would have a struggle taking care of two children on one income, and without anyone to even watch them without paying. And my opportunities were not the same as any other college graduate anymore. Virginia makes sure that you are marked and have little opportunity if you are ever convicted of a felony.

Anyway, I did my duty as a teacher at my new school, and made sure I reached the children who were having a hard time and I learned different ways to approach subjects so that they would be up to par with their classmates. I had a problem leaving anyone behind and generally did not leave anyone behind.

My children were enrolled in the local county schools. My daughter liked her school better than the ones near my old job and in Buckingham County where I had gone myself, and where I graduated. My children often visited the school where I taught and my son even made friends with some of the students there. I lived in a house beside the school, so I didn't even need to drive, although I did drive sometimes because of the number of things I needed to take with me into the classroom. Often, Harry worked two jobs: one as a cook, the other as a dishwasher. We stuck to our pact not to use. All was well and things were going smoothly. Harry had stepped into the role to be the father figure, especially to my son. I couldn't teach Dorian to be a man and I needed the man in my life to assume the role. Harry welcomed the opportunity and stepped right into it. My daughter was mostly reared by me, and my son by Harry.

We furnished the house nicely and were quite comfortable. We had been in the home for 3 months when Dorian's birthday came. He was 12 on October 20, 2000. Harry bought him a warm-up for his birthday, but told him to wait until he got the matching shoes before he wore it. Dorian was a good boy, often referred to as a nerd because he wasn't interested in some of the things the boys liked to do, but was very smart. He was content with his Play Station and only had 4 really close friends: his sister Sheba who was his best friend, his cousins James and Natalie and, a little boy named Kendrick. He sometimes did mischievous things to play tricks on us around the house. Mostly though, he played the playstation.

Then he played the most dangerous game I had ever seen: he ran in front of moving vehicles at the moment that they were close to him, darting across the road to get away at the last moment before a collision. When I first caught him playing the game, it was just before an 18-wheeler got to him and I really scolded him. The second time I spanked him. The third time was on Halloween, 11 days after his birthday. We had come home from school and the kids both did their homework. I was grading papers and Harry was at work. As we finished up, the children begged me to go trick or treating, since they knew that I was not going to our church to the alternative program, which was about 40 miles away. I wasn't going because I didn't have the gas money. It was a Tuesday and I didn't get paid until the next day. I said no a couple of times, then they reminded me how good they had been lately, first one then the other. So I said okay we would only go to a few areas then come back home. We first went to a subdivision that was fairly close to us. Then we went to a row of houses up on a knoll on the left. I dropped them off at the first house then drove to the end of the row.

We agreed that they wouldn't come down until they got to the end. Meanwhile I would drive to the other end. Well, I couldn't get into the drive because, apparently other parents had the same idea, and were in the driveway trying to come out. So I pulled over into an entrance to another drive on the other side of the road, but I didn't think that they could see me so I waited until the traffic behind me passed so I could get out of the car. By then I could see them coming down the knoll prematurely about 5 or 6 houses too soon. When got out of the car, my daughter was screaming "I think Dorian's hit! I think Dorian's hit!" We both began running to him. I said to Sheba, "If he got hit it won't be bad." That's before she said "that's Dorian's sneaker!" And we still had about a block to get to go to get to him. When we got to him I went straight down and knelt by him. I just shook him from his chest while calling his name. I was afraid to move him because thick blood was coming from the back of his head. There was a paramedic on the scene before the ambulance got there. People around me moved me so the paramedic could work.

I remember still trying to get to him. I kept crying, "No Lord, not now. Not yet, Not yet! He's only a baby, Lord, it's too soon." His eyes were open but they were vacant. I held on to hope because he was breathing as the paramedics continued to work on him. An officer suggested to me that I meet them at the hospital because they would be taking Dorian to the hospital about a mile away. I said I thought I could, so Sheba and I walked quickly walked back to the car and I drove to the hospital. I remember thinking while I was driving to the hospital that if Dorian survived he would be messed up and that there was no telling what he would need. I just knew that I needed my son. He had to survive. I called Harry as soon as I got to the hospital. He would be there in 10 minutes.

The ambulance got there first. The lights were off on the ambulance and I told Sheba that was a bad sign if it was Dorian's ambulance. A chaplain came over to me and asked me if there was anyone I wanted to call. I couldn't call anyone until I knew more about Dorian's condition. That was all that was important at the moment. I asked the chaplain "do we know about his condition? Is he still with us". He told me he didn't know.

Harry came and the chaplain kept telling us that he didn't know Dorian's condition. Harry just held on to me and kept me calm. The chaplain told Harry that I had not called my family and asked if he would call someone in the family. He was on the phone as I paced the floor. I didn't want him to call my Aunt because I knew she would blame me and I couldn't take that right now. He called her though.

After he made the calls, the chaplain said the doctors were ready to see us. He took us into a little room to wait for the doctor. It was likely only a few minutes that felt like an eternity before a doctor came into the room. All three of us held together tightly, the doctor said, "We did everything we could, but I'm sorry, Dorian has passed away.." I screamed agonized scream from the pit of my soul, feeling as though my son's life was being stripped from my womb and heart. I never knew I could make such a sound nor did I know anything could hurt so badly. I could scarcely breathe. I couldn't stand. All I could do was cry the pain in my heart and my soul. They say no pain is stronger than that of childbirth. Yes there is--the pain of the loss of a child.

It took us a while to take it all in. Harry and I also comforted Sheba who was understandably as distraught as well. We were taken to see his body and my knees began to give out. When we regained our composure, we left the room. We went back into the lobby where we saw that the Bishop of my church, my Aunt and the Pastor of the church where I taught school had come. Everyone wanted to know what happened, but I didn't want to talk to anyone. I did acknowledge and thank everyone for coming.

The pastor of the church where I taught called me back into the treatment area. He delicately explained that there was an opportunity here to give the corneas of Dorian's eyes for a waiting person and a child needing a heart valve to save his life and he asked if I would be willing to donate them from Dorian. I prayed about it.

My first instinct was not to touch my son's body. It seemed that I would be desecrating his body. Then I thought about Dorian and what he would want me to do. I could feel his generous heart saying, "Give them what they need, Mom. I can't use them anymore". And then I figured that those parts of him would live on even if I didn't know where. Someone would be looking through his eyes and I would spare another mother my fate with her child. So I agreed to donate.

When I got back home, I went to Dorian's room and just looked around. I opened the closet. The first thing I saw was the warm-up Harry had gotten for him. It was to be the first of many things that Harry was going to buy for him. Harry was going to teach Dorian to dress, and was about to buy sneakers for him with his next paycheck. He had been so ready to teach him the things about being a man that I could never teach him. That would not happen now. He was 12. He never wore the warm-up. We would give it to my nephew, James the next day who accepted it as though he was honored to have it.

It seemed that I was in a daze for the next few days. I just could not wrap my mind around the fact that Dorian was gone. I knew I see him again, but every time I thought about him it was just so incredulous to me that he was gone that I would be right back to the shocking, overwhelming and incredulous feeling that I had when I was first told he had passed. I kept trying to wrap my mind around the fact that he wasn't coming back. I didn't know what to do with myself.

People started coming by from the school giving their condolences and bearing gifts. I tried my best to say the right things to show how thankful I was, even though I felt really detached from everything. It was almost like I was going through the motions with someone speaking for me. Every prayer we had shook me back to myself for a while so I stayed in prayer lots of times so I could just get through the next minute, the next hour of accepting the death of my child. I talked to God all day and all night, asking him to please heal me, my heart enough to go on. There was a great weight in my spirit, a great pain that wouldn't go away. I cried a lot, and I had no desire to eat. The minister who was the principal of the school talked to me a lot when I saw her, and that helped me. I was grateful for her.

Going to see the body was hard. In fact every time I saw my son's lifeless body my knees weakened and I could hardly stand, from the time I first I saw him lifeless. I didn't know who picked the tie and shirt he wore but I knew I didn't like them. I also knew they were able to put something in place of his eyes, but they didn't. I started getting angry, but said nothing.

It was as though he was dealt with without delicacy to me. Even though I knew that funeral home had better limos, it seemed they used the "raggediest" one they had for me. I decided that it was best to put my complaints aside, so I left it alone until later. Even the eulogy I wrote was altered. And my aunt attempted to take every card I had received. It had to be brought to my attention. My mind was not there in cards and the money that would be in them. Harry got the pile from the funeral director, that were all addressed to me. Thank God he was there to catch me when I fell and to watch my back for people who would take advantage of me in the weakest, most vulnerable time of my life.

The funeral was a celebration. It was one befitting his life and I was even able to join in towards the end of the service. I even smiled at one point. I knew Dorian wouldn't want me to grieve so much but I couldn't help it. He was fine one minute and gone the next. I didn't know if my heart would ever heal, but I knew I would see him again and it would heal then, at least. Later, after I had returned to teaching I called the funeral home director to find out who had changed my eulogy because my Aunt said she didn't. I found out that the funeral director had not changed it and that it was more likely that the minister of the church who had observed that my children were with my Aunt for several years before my return had somehow tried to give my Aunt a credit that she had not sought and changed the eulogy. My cousin got the eulogy to me before the service and, though it upset me, I was prepared for the change before the service.

Teaching somehow had changed for me. Being around the students reminded me that my son was gone every day. We had joint classes when it came to religious teaching and I was always including my son in my part of the teaching. It didn't always go over well. I felt that I had to talk about Dorian. I guess it was to help with my grief. I really don't know why. Every time I thought of him, it was just like I was back at the time of his death. I was in shock of losing him, incredulous that he was gone all over again.

The holiday season was difficult: my first everything without him. We had not used since I left the preschool, but now Harry and I had begun using again periodically. Whenever I used I was in a zone devoid of pain. I would forget about everything. Using was the way I got through the pain of losing my mother especially, also my father. The loss of my mother was the closest pain to the pain of losing my son. But when I lost my mother, I was using mostly marijuana and some alcohol to numb the pain. Crack was a different animal. Crack changed you in a way that alcohol and marijuana never did. When you got up the next day you returned to yourself with alcohol and marijuana. But if you used crack regularly, it crept into your very being and eventually, you became a different person.

First of all you became depressed when you didn't have it and eventually, you stooped lower and lower to get it when you didn't have it or the money to buy it. Crack would become the only way to feel good and the feeling didn't last. Then every time I had any money, my stomach would flip and flip until I gave in and went to get it. Whenever I used regularly, I found myself taking care of my bills, buying some food, and going straight to it. So I didn't ever want to use regularly again. I didn't want to lose control of my life. Yet I used. I came to think of it as the devil's potion. It was something I decided not to buy again. I would do it only if it was given to me. I was teaching and I had my daughter to think about. I could not allow my character to be diminished. I told myself it was okay to use as long as I didn't do it often.

It was now April of the next year. What I didn't know was that Harry didn't have one of his jobs anymore. So while I was at work, he was using my car to go to Hampton Roads every day to help a dealer pick up a package. The dealer paid him every day and he was using every day. He would be at home upstairs in my room, which was the only room upstairs and I would be downstairs with Sheba. Since there were only men up there, I just left them to themselves. Once in a while Tom, the dealer would be there and give me a little something before he left. I would do it late. Sometimes I couldn't sleep until the wee hours of the morning. I began to notice that people were coming over more frequently, sometimes asking for Harry and sometimes for Tom and I began to think that some dealing was being done from my house. I was mortified as the house was a stone's throw from the school and I told Harry to put a stop to the traffic, and not to have Tom in the house anymore.

One day I was at work near the end of the day and I was asked to go to the Pastor's office. I was informed that the police were about to raid my house. I was told that drug activity had been ongoing at the house during the day for months, when I thought Harry was at work. I knew Harry had picked up Sheba from school by now, and the officers had me to call the house and have her come to the school. Then they raided the house, arresting everyone there. The house I lived in belonged to the church and I was fired. I would have 30 days to vacate. Another loss. I was devastated.

Chapter 15

Now I had lost my son and my job. I was depressed. Still I had to survive. Harry eventually got out because there was nothing found in the house. But I was still fired and we still had to get jobs. I was furious with Harry, yet I still loved him. I knew that my strongest attraction to him was because he was loyal and that I would never have to worry about him cheating on me. It just wasn't in his blood and that was rare. But I was also attracted to him because he used. That was because of my addiction, and because I had to be able to use in my relationships. Because my relationships started out with intoxicants and I normally drank or smoked marijuana before sex, alcohol and marijuana had become my way to enjoy sex.

When I smoked crack, sex was the farthest thing from my mind, though it often had the opposite effect on men. Fortunately, it affected Harry the same way it affected me. I knew that the reason I couldn't have sex without intoxicants was because of the abuses in my past. There was molestation as a child, rape in my early adult life and partial rape in my 30's. I was voluntarily sexually promiscuous in my 20's when I attended college, as I asserted my independence, choosing who to have sex with, as often as I wanted, with as many young men as I wanted. I was in the library whenever I wasn't in class so that I could. I maintained a 3.0 cumulative average and above and so I had my night life. And I always drank (and smoked marijuana, if I had it) before sex, even then.

Then I over drank sometimes and there were a few occasions that I blacked out and didn't remember who I had been with. Those were the days I felt violated. But it was my fault, so I sucked it up. I knew I was attractive and there would always be guys who would be trying to get next to me. But there was an emptiness in it as I saw couples forming and building together. But by my junior year, I met Rashad and I would also have a relationship to build on. There was still drinking every day that I was with him. It was not liquor, but mostly beer or wine during the week. But there was always some kind of alcohol around.

So the presence of alcohol in the bedroom had not changed. Harry and I were not nearly as sexually active as Rashad and I, so we only drank on days that we were intimate or getting high, which was not regularly for me.

When I got back to the house it was a wreck. They had torn up everything. It would be an all day job getting the house together. Sheba got her room together and I got the living room and kitchen back together. I decided to tackle the upstairs the next day. I would have to borrow my brother's steam cleaner to clean the carpets upstairs. Apparently, Harry had been using a gallon jug as a bathroom, according to the pastor, and it had spilled when they raided the house.

Over the next 30 days we cleaned the house and packed. We got jobs with a temp agency and began to save so we could move. We located a place and began to make payments on rent and deposit. Then on about the 28th day we began to move.

It was a trailer home on a small lake. It was spacious. It had 3 bedrooms and 2 bathrooms. This home was 5 miles out on the outskirts of town, though. One had to have a car to live in this rural area. At least my daughter could catch the bus to school, though. It was very quiet and peaceful. We settled in and looked for steady work. It would be months before I found a summer job. Harry was awaiting sentencing for some trouble he managed to get into.

However, he landed a construction job and later found out he would be able to work under the work release program so he could help me with the bills.

He and I continued to get high. It filled a void in my life, I told myself. We tried not to spend a lot of money getting high, and instead would loan out the car for crack. That went on for months with the same guy until one day we didn't get the car back. There had been a problem with the car leaking oil and the engine went with quarts of oil in the trunk. The guy didn't even bother to call us. Instead he left the car on an old lot where he allowed another guy to tow it and then he got somebody to pick him up. We had told him about the oil leak and told him to put oil in the car if the light came on. That oil was in the trunk. I guess he didn't pay attention and the engine locked up.

We tried to get a motor for it and it took a long time. Meanwhile the car sat. Long story short, the guy who owned the lot began stripping it for parts and I just lost the car altogether. So now we were walking. But I needed transportation and had to get a car from somewhere. I ended up getting a car from a private lot. It was a 20-25-year-old mustang in 2001. I made a payment of half of the $500 purchase price. The car ran well but started to fall apart after a couple weeks. One of the doors to this 2-door car started opening only from the inside. Other things began to rattle. Then the muffler started making noise. I always had to do something to the car. I had to get a bootleg inspection. Even he didn't pass it for inspection. I would end up never being able to get an inspection on the car. This would be the car that caused all the trouble.

Harry had to appear in court about a traffic incident that occurred on the night of Dorian's funeral. If I hadn't sent him out for some feminine products, he wouldn't have been in the car. He had some issues with his license. We had delayed and delayed the court date because I needed Harry around to help me get into another place, since he had been quite instrumental in helping me loose the other home. And my job. And my car.

He had to serve time but would be given the work release program for the duration of his sentence. In order for him to have work release he would have to be picked up every morning by someone who would take him to work and drive him back to jail after work. The "hoopdi" mustang would be the car. No inspection sticker and all. I really wondered how long I was going to make it with this car, period. Sooner or later, the car was going to be pulled over and I would start to accumulate tickets.

I was picking Harry up and dropping him off for months. And I had begun to get tickets for not having an inspection sticker. One night I was driving with one headlight because I didn't have money to fix it. I had already dropped Harry off, and I had had a glass of wine. I was headed home. The only way for me to display 2 headlights was to turn on my high beams, so when a driver from the opposite side of the street blinked his lights to have me dim my lights, I did not respond because I didn't need a cop to stop me because of my single headlight.

It turned out that a cop was the one blinking his lights, so he flipped around and pulled me over. He told me that my lack of response was an indicator that I may be drinking and driving. Well, if I knew that would be the assumption with a cop, I would have dimmed the lights. I guessed I would chalk it up as experience: now I knew. I called a new friend to pick up my daughter and take her home. Diane knew and had sung in a group with my eldest brother, Eric and she lived within walking distance of our house. I had met her while we didn't have a car. When she came the tow truck came as well.

The car was towed because they smelled the wine. I had my first DUI. I blew a .09. Now I would have to find the money for tow and get somebody to bond me out. My brother Eric came to get me around 10pm. He took me home and paid the impound fee so I could get the car in the morning. I couldn't get my car in time to get Harry when he was supposed to go to work. He was mad about it. That meant he wouldn't be out for the day. I was mad because he was supposed to get another ride back and couldn't get that ride, so now I was on the road after having a drink. Now I had a criminal charge that I had to go to court to resolve.

I continued to look for work which was hard because of the lack of available jobs in the area. I kept my application active at the temporary agency. I got a summer job as director of a preschool, which was near where I lived, so I didn't have to go into town to work. Harry got out having served his time for driving that night that I asked him to go out. So he was now home. The job he had while on work release ended and now he was looking for work. It was rough. We were living hand to mouth. As soon as I got money, it had to go out for something. I found myself over at Diane's house a lot. We would have some wine or beer and on occasion, we got high. Harry would sometimes be at the home of some people we knew, who had recently moved into the neighborhood. That wasn't good all the time because there was no telling what he and the man of that house would get into. He sometimes sold drugs and no telling what else, but they left me in peace, so I was okay.

I did learn that Bill, the guy he was hanging with, would be at our house along with another guy and his stepson of about 12 years old. Since the child was there, I supposed everything was okay. Sheba was there and Harry protected her like a father always. She would also tell me what went on if there was anything to tell. I understood that the reason they came over was because we had air conditioning and they did not. I had air conditioning because my brother, Eric bought it for me. I surely did not have the money for it. The summer went on and got hotter. By the end of the summer when my job ended, Harry had been arrested again. I found out that there were some other things that he did not answer for that he did not tell me about and this time he would be taken back to Hampton Roads to answer for them. I had no idea what they were. So here I was. Not even with a car now. I had been stopped on other occasions and they impounded the car because it was in ill repair. I would not get my brother to pay it this time because it would only be impounded again. I got Diane to take me to social services to find rental aid and so I could go to the unemployment office. The Trade Center bombings also happened around that time. I had been taking a nap on the couch. When I saw the first building smoking, I thought it was a movie for a moment, then realized, like the rest of the nation that it was really happening.

A woman who worked with social services came to me at the house a few days later. She seemed to be a godsend because she told me she would get me a job and get me into an apartment complex in town, through a friend, so that I could get around. Over the next month, I got the apartment. The complex rented by income, so whenever I wasn't working, there was no rent. The job they came up with for me was a chicken house worker. But I felt like it didn't matter as long as I had work. But that was before I went for my first day.

Chapter 16 - The Chicken House

When I got there I sat in a huge room that was apparently where we ate. The smell was not unbearable but it was clearly there. It was the smell of live chickens and I wondered if I would ever be able to eat there. But once I went in the back where the first of the rows were, the smell was so overwhelming that I became nauseated. It was a mixture of chicken feathers and chicken feces and the slight smell of ammonia. As the slight and petite lady handed me gloves and a wagon, she explained to me that my first job was to "pull my dead". That meant that I was to go down each row and pull all the chickens that had died overnight from the cages. Now the cages stacked from the floor about four. They were all adjoining cages, maybe 20 to 24 inches in width, depth, and height, and the rows were so long I couldn't see the other end of the rows.

The cages were on both sides of each row, unless it was the first or last row. There were at least 6-8 rows to each chicken house. The floor was open beneath the cages so that the chicken feces would fall to the floor beneath the one that we were on. There were 4-6 chickens in each cage and I had never seen so many chickens in my life. This was the dispensary. The chickens laid eggs, and the eggs rolled out of each cage and onto a conveyer belt that was constantly in motion, moving the eggs to their next location. The walk down the first aisle was my worst. The further down I walked, the more intense the smells became. I was wearing a surgical mask, yet the smell was still strong. As I spotted dead chickens, I pulled them out.

I hurried as fast as I could, checking both sides as I went. Some of the chickens looked deformed when I took them out and one died with the egg only halfway out of it. It seemed so inhumane that they fed and fed the chickens and they laid and laid eggs in those small boxes cramped together until they died. When I got to the end of the row, I finally could remove my mask and breathe. I wouldn't dream of taking it off before I got to the end because if the ammonia smell didn't kill me, the very fine feathers that were in the air constantly, would. After I had pulled all my dead there was a hole in front of the row, where the work prep area was. I was to drop them in that hole. I had felt so nauseated at times that I nearly vomited on several occasions but I was assured it would pass along with the lightheadedness I was feeling.

My next job was to sweep the rows because of the coating of the feathers on the row floors. By the time I had done that it was time for me to leave. I was glad I didn't have to eat there. I decided that I would eat before work or not eat until I got home and bathed. I would try it both ways. I would try not eating before I went to work and see if I was more or less nauseous, because I had eaten before going to work that day. Turned out I was better off not eating until I was at home and clean. The smell stayed in my work clothes. My daughter kept bringing it to my attention.

I left my boots there in a locker everyday, as recommended. It wasn't until I saw the floor under the one where I worked that I knew the real reason to leave my boots there. I saw three to four foot high piles of chicken feces as long as the rows of chickens. I saw them as part of the tour of the facility and was informed that sometimes it would also be my job to clear the rows of water and feces between the rows. As though the rows upstairs were not enough, now there was this new low. My breathing became more labored each day that I worked, and I wondered how it was possible for a person to continue to work there for years as some of the workers claimed that they had. How could they even maintain their dignity? Mine took a hit every day that I worked there.

I couldn't quit, because if I did I would lose my food stamp benefit. I brought home less than $100 a week in this part time job. I sank to a new low on what would be my last day. Today, I had to sweep the rows down below. Rows of chicken feces 3-4 feet high. The taller the rows were the more the rows became obstructed. I put on two masks and went down my first row and my eyes watered. On more than one occasion, I nearly fell. Had I fallen in it I surely would have been sick. I could see the maggots swimming in it, and I was scared the whole time I worked in the area. I was lightheaded and I had to take many breaks in order to finish.

I made my decision then to see a doctor to be medically discharged from the position. I would actually have to attend a hearing before social services would accept the fact that I could no longer work there. But I was out! Yes! I lost 2 pair of work boots that I left in a locker for whatever unfortunate individual who found himself working there and could fit them.

Now I found myself at the unemployment office pretty regularly in order to keep my benefit. But there was little to no work available in the area and it seemed quite fruitless most times.

Months went by and I got help from my family to pay bills sometimes and I still got high when I could. Mostly I would invite people over who had money to get me high. It was my only indulgence, my only escape from my miserable life; broke, busted with no end to it in sight.

I was still in contact with Harry and my deposition for the case involving the death of my son would be happening soon. Harry was out of jail and called me a few times a week. I loved him, I think more for his loyalty than anything. Loyalty like his was hard to find and I was too broken in my spirit to see that he was the worst thing for me. I just wanted to feel good because I felt bad all the time because of the state of my life. I had Sheba so I always made sure she never saw what I was doing, but she knew. She also knew that before Harry, I didn't do it. But I was still not well, and with or without Harry, I would likely start getting high again at some point in my life. Why? Because getting high filled a void that nothing else filled in me. I wouldn't understand what was really missing in my life that caused me to return to my "old standby" of getting high to feel good, for years.

We had the deposition and we knew things could go either way. My lawyers continued to negotiate a settlement for me. My concern was that I had no work and little money was coming in. I still had to pay utilities and cable and I had only a $200 check to survive on each month, which didn't cover my bills. The best I could do was pay on my bills and pray for the settlement to come sooner than later.

My asking my family, mainly my brother Alexis, for money was getting old, and they were tired of it. Harry wanted to come as soon as I got the settlement and I told him he could as long as he got a job. In the meantime I continued to look for work. The day came when it was eminent that I was going to lose my electricity. I contacted my lawyer asking if I could borrow from the firm so I could hold out for more money. I was informed that it was illegal for them to help me, so I informed them that we needed to settle because I was in dire straits.

Though my attorneys wanted me to hold out, I was not in the financial position to do that. I was told that the maximum settlement would be $36,000 because of the amount of insurance the driver was covered for under his insurance. The whole issue had been because Virginia has a law involving contributory negligence, meaning that if a person is even 1% responsible for his own demise, he cannot collect on a lawsuit. As far as I was concerned, the insurance company could never pay me enough money for my son. Right now, if they could just get me out if this jam, I would be okay.

So, within a couple of weeks, I had my settlement. It was a little over $8000, and my daughter would have $2500 held by the courts until she was 18, and the balance of my benefit was paid to the funeral home. The lawyers got the rest.

I immediately overpaid all of my bills, such that he projected new bills would be covered also. I had my younger sister to hold on to

$2000 for me, and I went shopping for things I needed and had been unable to buy. I gave my daughter some money (around $200) more than once. I went grocery shopping and I went with some people I knew for most of the night where I could get high that first day. My stomach had been flipping all day, while I was taking care of business. I ended up telling Harry I received the settlement when I was half-asleep and the next thing I knew, he was there. His appetite for crack had always been more intense than mine because I used an ash bowl, while he used the glass stem, which was a much more concentrated hit. I didn't use the stem because I could never get the hang of it. By the time I saw smoke, I was out of breath trying to get it going. So I made the ash bowl, which was what I learned to smoke on in the first place. With it you put fire to the crack, which set atop some ashes and pulled it straight through a makeshift pipe. To me that simplified things, and I didn't get so intensely high. To tell the truth, I would get so afraid of my racing heart that I would take breaks, while it didn't seem to bother others to just hit back-to-back.

I had also developed a paranoia back in Richmond and had now begun to hide my hitter after I hit. Before that first hit, everything was fine. After the first hit, I feared that the police were going to kick the door in at any moment. That's throughout the high. That's another reason I would take breaks: so I could lose the feeling that the police were coming, long enough to hit again.

After Harry came, the money started to go fast. He wanted to get high much more often than I did. And I just kept shelling out the money even though sometimes the high was too much for me and I would stop and let him have it. He had started hanging at Sharon's house where he would buy crack and smoke. He had his own hustle, sometimes and not get money from me. I tried to keep up appearances around Sheba, and she was another reason I didn't want to get high sometimes. But, of course my stomach would flip whenever crack was around. In a month or so, I was down to the money that I had my sister hold and I asked for it back. We did some responsible things like pay the bills, even though Harry wanted to flip it instead. And at the end if a couple of weeks, that was gone too.

I heard about a job at a sewing factory that made military bags and other items. So I applied for and got that job. It was tedious work because you did the same thing all day. It was boring and I don't think I was fast enough for them, but it was work and it came with a paycheck. It wasn't full time, though. I worked and Harry was supposed to be looking for work. In my off times, we found schemes like boosting to support our habits, because I was not going to lose my place. If the utilities got cut off, you had to have them back on in 24 hours or lose the apartment. So I wasn't spending any money until I paid them. When I got my settlement, social services cut me off altogether, saying they wouldn't be able to give me aid again until the time lapsed that would be equal in aid to the amount of my settlement, or the next calendar year.

Harry and I managed to rack up a charge for some televisions. I also got a charge for some cell phones. Harry would have also been caught, but he managed to elude the police.

So now I had a few charges that I would eventually have to answer for, along with my DUIs. But they released me on my own recognizances, since I was not a flight risk and had never failed to appear in court. One day I was at work and when I got off the bus I was met by one of the residents at the complex where I lived, and I was told that the police had run up into my house and that they had taken Harry. I went to my apartment first and on the way up the stairs, my second floor neighbor confirmed that my place had been run into and told me that the resident manager wanted her to tell me to come to the office the minute I got home.

After I looked over the apartment, I went to the office. The resident manager told me first that she knew about my settlement money and that I had not reported the income. She had also known about some of the get high activities I was having and that she had known for some time that Harry was living in my apartment. Then she dropped the bomb that I knew was coming: since police, especially the Federal Marshalls, had run up into my house to get Harry, I would have to move. I had 30 days to get it done.

Now I thought Harry was out of jail. Apparently he had skipped bond in a pending case and came to my house. Thanks a lot Harry, I said to myself. I made my decision not to let him back into my life again that very day. I didn't know where I was going to go. I prayed that for the first time in a long while for God to help me. He did.

I ended up across from the shopping center in town. It was an older building with another tenant upstairs. The set up was kind of strange. Each room had a door leading to the next room, straight in a row. So to get to the living room from my room, I had to pass through Sheba's room. And to get to the bathroom from the living room, I had to pass through the kitchen. There were three doors leading from the apartment to the hall (one in each room), and I had a storage space next door to me with a separate lock. I didn't really care for the set up, but considered myself blessed with it. It was a good building in a great location. I was happy to have a place to go. I moved out on time from the other apartment and into the new one. Only a few people knew where I moved. I wanted to keep it that way. I had decided not to communicate with Harry anymore. He kept too much information away from me that I needed to know if he was going to be at my house. Now there were two residences that I had lost as a direct result of his activities. And they were activities I knew nothing about like he and Tom taking my car practically every day to Hampton Roads to buy drugs and like being wanted by the police and not telling me that, knowing I was in a by-income apartment. I wasn't having him causing me to lose again.

It turns out that two of the few people who knew where I lived would be the cause of me losing the place I was now in. Apparently, Sharon and James, two people I knew from my last apartment went and robbed some storage spot on Longwood's College Campus. I allowed them to store some things in my storage spot. The landlord had a camera in the storage unit, unbeknownst to me. So I'm guessing there was some kind of tip and the police ended up coming to my house and knocking on the door. Before they came, James came and was trying to get the things out. He had gotten a few things out, so they caught him there and arrested him. It was then that I knew for sure there was a camera.

The guy upstairs confirmed it, and the police knew I didn't have my hand on the goods at all. Well, now after just a few months, I was out of there too. I went from Harry getting me kicked out to two other people getting me kicked out. Why, because they got me high with whatever money they came up with by whatever means. The hunt for a place to live was on again. I had only been in that place for a couple of months.

The next place was a house. It wasn't in good shape, but it was a place to stay. I had to scrub the place from top to bottom. I did like my room, the attic room. The living room was kind of small, but I had a place to stay. I borrowed the money from my younger brothers to pay for it because this time I couldn't put it together in the little time that I had to move.

It was only a few weeks before I finally got a job at the local radio station. I would be doing some clerical work, light bookkeeping and going to local businesses and selling advertising on the station for their businesses. There would be no bus to the location from the main road, but I knew I would have a ride for now. After that I would have to walk from the main road, which was about a half mile. I didn't care. I needed the work. I also needed to pay the rent.

The time was coming for me to go to court and actually face the charges of theft and DUI and I informed my employer of the court dates and was honest about why I was in court. I went on about my clerical duties. I called businesses on the phone to try and set up appointments with owners and managers. I would have to walk to each business so I wanted to schedule 2-3 appointments and walk into as many businesses each day as I could. I was also taught how to make commercials and would end up making commercials for most of the clients I had. One of my favorite clients was a lady named Dee, who ran a braid shop. We would become friends. Going to her shop was a welcome break from the heat during my work day.

In facing my charges, the DUI's came first. I was given weekends for several weeks. And I completed that. My daughter was becoming quite responsible and I trusted her at home with her best friend, whom I had allowed to become a part of our family since she was having problems at home. Her grandmother agreed with the arrangement. I had no problems with her when she had visited, so I agreed. She helped out a little with expenses so it was a win-win situation. Then came the charges for theft.

My lawyer, thank God for him, had gotten work release for me. I would be out from morning around 10:00 to not later than 9:00 pm. For the most part, the guy who worked the overnight shift would come and get me from the jail in the morning. Getting a ride back was something that I worked out day by day. I noticed one day after work that the lady at the braid shop either had the same name as a work release inmate or was a work release inmate because one of the property baskets had her name on it. When I saw her the next day, I asked her if she did work release because I thought I saw her name on a basket when I went in. She admitted she was on work release and agreed to bring me back at night. That was a relief! I no longer had to worry about getting back to the jail.

I was really impressed with my daughter's ability to follow directions and take the money that I gave her to pay the bills when I was not at home, and to clean the house. She also went school, did her class work and brought her report card home. I was so proud of her. I surely couldn't be there and I couldn't pay anyone else to be there. I had asked the lady across the road to check on my daughter and her friend from time to time and make everything was okay. If I didn't get my daughter, I would call Carol and make sure that all was well. Things went well while I was on work release. I had built up monthly accounts from local business owners that more than doubled my salary and was receiving and recording payments. I was getting more accounts as well, but not with the same frequency. Most of the time I was at the station alone unless Rick came by, who was the one who actually put a word in and got me the job. I liked being alone, without the boss because I had freedom of movement. Most people recorded their shows, anyway, so the station ran itself. And there was never a day that I didn't leave the station, unless the weather was bad. I wasn't crazy about walking long distances in the rain.

The day came that I would answer for my last charge. At the hearing, I had to bond out. My time was almost up for the work release and I was bonded out by my brother, Alexis. Though the station owner said he would bond me out, he didn't. He was shocked to see me walking in the door with my sister. He needed to pay me my last check! When he saw how serious I was, he paid me.

Apparently, the station was now under new management. I continued to work there for a while until new management turned the station to a streaming Latter Day Saints satellite station that just ran with no onsite intervention. We talked about doing a live show with local participants to showcase their talents to justify an income for me, but it was only a couple of hours per day. That wasn't going to be enough to support us, so when I wasn't at the station, I was looking for work. I was out of work for the most part for a couple months when Carol told me about the factory where she worked. The pay was good for that area, and the factory had just started hiring again.

So I made my way to it and filled out an application and I got the job. My rent was backed up and I had a court date to resolve it. The landlord did not want to work with me even with the new job, so I had to apartment hunt again. Derek, I guy that got high with, told me about an apartment in a great location. It was a privately owned duplex. It was a good looking place from the outside, and was an older building. It had the smallest kitchen I had ever seen. But it had 2 full bathrooms and 2 bedrooms and it was a place to go. I would have to negotiate to pay the rent with my first check and hoped that I could. I would be working 7 days a week for the first month, maybe more, so I should be able to handle it. The landlord agreed and I had to pay rent and deposit with my first check. So we moved to the new apartment. We both had our own bathroom which was great. The location was great and I was easily able to arrange a ride to and from work.

The job was good. It was tedious work, like most factory work was, but it would pay the bills. When I got the check, it was barely enough to pay the landlord and my ride. I went to the landlord with the check and showed it to him asking if I could take a little money to survive on, but he kept me to the agreement. So I was broke for another 2 weeks. It was a long 2 weeks. Rent would be due again in another couple of weeks, so I would be paying the rent again when I got paid. This time it would just be the one rent though, so I could swing that.

During my time there Derek came by sometimes but not frequently. I decided to slow down on getting high. I drank wine practically daily to have some kind of buzz. I worked from 3-11p.m. daily and after a month or so, it became tiresome not having a break from work. I dealt with it. Getting high was one of the ways I dealt with it. I had a friend whose house I would go over and get high. He was a dealer and I could stay for hours and he would give me crack in exchange for sexual favors. Of course, I couldn't wait until he finished, so I could get on with the business of getting high. I must say that he gave more than he got. I might smoke $200 and give him very little in return. Sometimes I would simply put some crack on my tab and pay him when I got paid.

Other than that, I would work and come home and relax, having some wine if I could. I never had to worry about Derek pressuring me for sex. He had a foot fetish and got off on my walking around in heels and stepping on things. As long as he was spending money, I didn't have a problem with it.

The time came for the company urinalysis. They gave me notice when I got off from work that the next day would be my day. I had already bought a product to clear my urine in advance of the test. Mostly, near the time of the test, I had smoked marijuana because I was on narcotic medication for a tooth, but I had a little crack a couple of days before, as well. It was also going to be payday that day, so I would be running around. In my haste to take care of my business, I forgot to take it before leaving the house. By the time I got back home, it was 3 hours before work and I would have to be at the testing center by 2:30 or be fired for a no-show. I hoped it would work. By the look of the urine in the cup, I was still very dirty. It was as though all the toxins had washed down and were just exiting.

A few days later, I was fired. Well, there went another loss. I was done with the whole area and wanted to return home to D.C. At my first available opportunity, I made plans to do just that. I made arrangements with the mother of my daughter's closest friend for a place to stay to allow her to finish high school. I would bring her to D.C. when she finished next year (2004). So I called information and got the number for Teddy's aunt because I knew she would know where he was. Surely he would know where I should concentrate my efforts. It was great talking to him. I still loved him. When I left him and went to school, I still missed him. I knew that he still saw other women who were older than me when I was with him, though, and it hurt. I think that's why I felt justified in beginning another relationship with Rashad while I was in school. I could say, though, that Teddy had been a good provider. Even though I worked, he always left money in the house that I had access to for whatever we needed. I had heard that Teddy would use heroin and cocaine and "speedball" but I had never even seen him with drugs. I respected that he kept it away from me if he did it.

The most I was doing while with him was smoke a joint and maybe drink a beer. Because I knew I was in competition with other females, I ran a mile every morning before work and did my yoga to keep myself in shape. The last time I saw him he visited the house where I lived, and since Rashad refused to leave, I had to let him know about the relationship. Teddy stayed downstairs in the house and before he left, he still gave me money, though I had tried to turn it down. I think Teddy thought I was going to get over Rashad and be back with him in the end. At the time I thought I might as well. Anyway, in the conversation I told him that I did still love him and I had never stopped loving him, but right now I was trying to come back to D.C. I wanted him to help me find a job by giving me suggestions about what jobs I should seek.

He knew my background and suggested that I should first try a job that was pretty wide-open in the area right then, one in telemarketing. So while still living in Virginia, I began looking for jobs by getting the D.C. paper from a store that I knew had them. I began talking to some employers, letting them know that I would be in the area soon. Some of them scheduled tentative times to interview based on when I could get there. When my brother Douglas had to go up to the area anyway, he agreed to take me. He put me up in the hotel for the night along with him. Douglas thought it was a bad plan, but it was the only plan that I thought would actually work.

I went to Teddy's job the next day. He looked basically the same. I was glad to see him. We embraced, kissed. The flame was still there. But he now had his own family: a wife and son. I wasn't the family wrecking type, so the time we spent today would be our only time. He had already asked an older gentleman that he knew to put me up temporarily so that I could job search. I also had the number for a place to go to an interview for a place to stay, once I got a job. It was a family member of Sheba's friend. Deb had a husband and 2 sons. We had a sit-down and the arrangement seemed like it would work out just fine. It went well. I felt like an extension of the family. My hours were from 12-9pm. So I only spent significant time there on the weekends. There were mandatory Saturdays twice a month as well. But it was good. I trained and became one of the best in the office. We did our telemarketing, calling homeowners, gathering their personal information hopes of getting them to refinance. It paid well and I was easily able to meet my rent each month.

After about a month, Deb confided in me that she had also had a crack addiction. She went to outpatient treatment daily. One day she wanted to get high. I shared that I had an addiction to it too and that I was trying to stay away from it. After about an hour we both succumbed to our addictions. Feeling really bad about using, I retreated to my room.

I would find out how much worse her addiction was than mine. She couldn't stop. It would be the middle of the night before she would stop. Her husband would now know that we had gotten high. I think I had better control because I didn't use a stem. Everybody I knew who did use one went out of control. I was glad I didn't like them. They were too potent for me and I was always afraid of my heart racing, so I would take ibuprofen or drink alcohol to calm myself. One thing was for sure, I was beginning not to like the high as much anymore. The paranoia, the getting crack that wasn't always good, the spending more money because of it, the looking around on the floor for imaginary pieces that might have dropped, the frustration of missing the hit, all made me begin to not like it, but I had a compulsion to use it anyway. My stomach would flip and I would think about it until I used. When I didn't use, I wanted to or Deb would use and I would use with her.

One day, a coworker gave me a ride home and offered to take me to his church. I had talked to him about my addiction and he confided that he, too, was struggling with his addiction to crack. Church was helping him. I would go because I needed help and I was curious about what he was learning that I didn't know that was helping him. I also needed God back in my life. I hadn't been to church for a few years.

So I started attending his church. It was a small, intimate setting, and I enjoyed it. Before long, I began teaching Sunday school as I had in Virginia before I met Harry. But there were times that I didn't go and times that J didn't go, so church was not as effective as it could have been had I gone regularly.

It would be another year before I would start to go regularly. Then, because I ended up moving to Maryland and so far away from the church in D.C., we would lose touch and I would stop attending church again. But I had begun to learn things I didn't know, so I knew that church was a good place to be and that I would eventually return to that church in particular.

Chapter 16

Sheba graduated from high school. And over the following year, she had completed a course of study in cosmetology. We had tried to get her in Norfolk State, but when I went to Richmond a week late because I had previously agreed to house and baby sit for my boss so she could go out of town, there was no available housing. This was the trip when I first met this boyfriend of my daughter's. I had now become a mortgage loan officer and was in better company. I actually lived, at the time, with my boss and her family. I had stopped using and I felt better about my life, and I was away from "the hood" and the constant temptation to use.

I had great successes as a loan officer after a slow start. I had several closings in a month's time and was financially able to leave my boss' house. I ended up first taking over the lease of boss' relative because of the difficulty in finding a place near the job.

This time my daughter would be with me along with her boyfriend. They actually came before I left my boss' house, and moving was necessary because her boyfriend had a problem with authority and was not following the rules of the house. He was also disrespectful to my boss at times. I had initially let him come where I was because he had taken my daughter to New York and, even though they were having a hard time surviving, she refused to leave him. I was afraid for her. She had lived in rural Virginia all of her life, save some time she lived in Richmond, now she was in New York! I knew New York, and I knew my daughter was "green" even though she didn't think so. Letting him come with her was the only way she would come to where I was. It was the lesser of two evils, so I would do it at least temporarily. But I would live to truly regret letting him into my home.

Chapter 17

One of my clients was a real estate agent and I assisted him in saving the homes of a couple of his clients, and got him paid significant amounts for the part he played in purchasing the homes under foreclosure and returning the ownership to the original owners.

That agent allowed me to rent a vacant house under his control, so long as I kept the property clean and showed the house to prospective buyers whenever he informed me that they would be coming by to view the property. That worked out fine for me. Besides, there would an opportunity for me to close another loan if the property went under contract. Sheba and her boyfriend had the basement area. There was a bathroom downstairs so they were downstairs most of the time. The problem was that they began to have a lot of people over and that wasn't going to work.

Sheba took his side in whatever discussions we had, and I was beginning to see that she was being brainwashed by him. The daughter who never took any mess from any guy was now beginning to take sides with a guy who had no problem disrespecting his elders and authority figures. I let him stay but made him understand that he had to follow the rules so I could do what I was supposed do as a resident of the house, showing the house to prospective buyers.

That meant no company and no smoking weed in the basement during specified hours when people would be coming to see the house. I bought air fresheners and they bought incense. I had better not ever smell weed in the house. As much as I wanted my daughter to be with me until she could be on her own, they could both leave before I would have to leave for not doing what I was supposed to do. I guess he got it through his head as well as did Sheba. Except for the fact that nobody had a job but me, they behaved tolerably well for the rest of the time that we were there.

There was something that went on at the house between C (Sheba's boyfriend) and the agent's brother who had come to do repairs and upgrades in the basement. I knew C and I knew he likely disrespected the man in some way so I cleared the disagreement as best as I could. Eventually, there was one buyer who seemed to be a good prospect, but for some reason, his paperwork didn't go through, even though he had good credit. The second buyer was apparently going to go through and I would be asking the agent to help me out with a new place so that I could vacate this one.

The buyer for this property would not be doing his loan through me because he had already used someone else to work up his loan. They wanted to take possession so soon that I didn't have time to find a place. The agent actually put us up in a hotel and put our belongings in storage for a few days until we could find a place. We found a house in a good location in Silver Spring, but it was about 5 good blocks from mass transit. It was the upstairs of a single-story home. There was a downstairs tenant. There was a kitchen and a separate entrance with bathroom as well, so we didn't have to see each other unless we were doing laundry. The house had been remodeled and there were three bedrooms. There was a patio with a table and lawn chairs and a fenced-in backyard.

I loved the house. I hadn't closed loans lately with Monie's company and going to work there was too far away. I decided to find work closer by I had completed my 40-hour course for licensing but needed to pay nearly $500 for the test to be licensed. So I needed to close some loans. I got a number of clients who wanted fixed-rate mortgages, but they all dragged their feet. I had warned them of the current trend and that people were losing value in their homes, and they should act now. Not only did they need to take heed to what I was saying, I was also in trouble with the rent because I had no closings in the past few months and desperately needed a closing. By the time they all decided to act, it was too late. Their homes lost value, and they had no equity to refinance.

Sheba and C were looking for work and still had people regularly coming over who would sometimes be at the house when I got home. I saw Eric, a guy I worked with when I was telemarketing mortgages, one day and he told me about a place near me where I could work telemarketing home exterior products, so I applied there to work part-time evenings. At least I would have a weekly income. Unfortunately, my income would not cover my rent of $1400 per month even if I gave it all to my landlord.

I told both Sheba and C about the job. They both got jobs there. Sheba lasted much longer than C, who would not be as reliable about staying and doing his shift as she and I were. C had really become a burden and became increasingly territorial as though the house was his, and tried to tell me what to do in my own house. We argued regularly and I feared at one time that I would kill him in his sleep. Sometimes I got through to him and sometimes I let it go. Sheba still loved him even though he would sometimes talk to other females and I continued to let him stay.

I know that I had a guilty conscience about leaving my children with my aunt for several years, and not being in their lives for so long. I wanted Sheba to be happy and to be able to say that I was doing for her in her adult life and making up for not being there those years when she was a minor. That was a big part of why I continued to let him stay, I knew the other part was that I now had a much lower opinion of myself and as an addict, had tolerated abuses from him, neighbors, friends and family because I was now lesser of a person because they knew I had the addiction problem. And family didn't trust me, generally, even though I never took from them. They also knew I had been to jail and I felt I shamed my family in a way that no one else in the family had. I had not become a success for any serious length of time. I had had good jobs in the beginning like senior secretary and legal secretary, but that was at the beginning of my addiction, when I still strongly felt that I was somebody and was going to be someone who was great. Now I was just happy to be successful as a loan officer but it seemed that no loans would close as houses lost value and bankers stopped lending like they had been lending.

Over the time I had lived in his house for at least 8 months without paying the rent. I eventually gave up on going to the office unless I had something to enter into my system. It was stressful. I had been to court twice. But we all knew that the landlord was not going to evict anyone. Most often, so we were told, she wouldn't even show up to court. We had an opportunity to live rent-free for a while to fix things and I wanted to leave the house, so that we wouldn't continue to take advantage of the landlady. So we moved to Hagerstown, stored our things there in the garage.

This would be one of Sheba and C's friends, who had 4 children. It was a 5-bedroom house with basement. Two of Jule's children bunked together, so there was room upstairs for Sheba and C to take a room. I slept on the couch. The house was comfortable and spacious. I was sure to clean the downstairs, cook and wash dishes as many times as needed per day to sort of earn my keep. We were there through the summer. I was tiring of being there because I was around C every day and because being there, I was not able to work. For one thing, I would not be able to get to a job in this rural area without a car. I needed to find someplace I could stay and go back to the D.C. area. This being without an income was not for me.

A new neighbor who had moved to the area was interviewing in Silver Spring and Rockville and I asked if I could use that opportunity to return to the D.C. area. It worked out. I had about a week at a friend's until I would need my own place to go. I would have to work fast to get work and a place to stay.

I would end up going to my last mortgage office, which was taking too much time and was not lucrative. One of the loan officers had an aunt who offered to let me stay a while, then she decided she'd rather not wait until I got paid, out of the blue one day. The real estate agent who had helped me so much in the past, and whose pockets I had helped to line, introduced me to an agent who worked with him, when I called him needing a place to stay. She was not able to really help me there. I let my friend, Cole know that I had nowhere to go, suddenly, so he said to come on back.

The agent, Neta, was able to help me to earn some money, though. Eventually, she had a house I could go to temporarily, and there would be room for Sheba and C, who by now were also ready to return to the area. Either they took longer to become frustrated or Jule had become tired of them. This time Sheba was pregnant. She was intent on finding her own now, for her child. I would try to stay away from the house as much as possible this time since Neta had Cole and I working together and usually picked us up for work at his place. I would hold Sheba responsible for the house and stay mostly at Cole's.

C had brought dogs that left feces in the basement. I had already said the dogs couldn't come with them, that they should leave the dog and litter in rural Hagerstown. But they didn't know there would be a problem with Neta. We had to go because a permanent tenant was coming and I had everything put in storage. The Sheba and C returned to Hagerstown and Cole and I continued to work until the work ran out. I ended up going to New Jersey and staying with relatives, which was probably a good move for the moment.

I would reconnect with the church. I had held on to much of the written information that we had studied in church in D.C. One thing that I had not done, which was continually done amongst the other members in the church in D.C, was that they memorized and meditated on the Word of God. I had never done that and saw no reason to start now. It didn't stop me from learning that I hadn't memorized it. And some of it was committed to memory because I had heard it so often. I began to study all the information that I had when I was settled in New Jersey. I went back and started to record verses on cards as I had begun to do in D.C. I kept notes from the sermons in D.C. The scripture referred to in many of the sermons spoke to me specifically in my heart. I began to memorize the scriptures because doing so seemed to make a difference to the other members and I felt that their knowledge and understanding was increased because of it. I had learned so much that I didn't know before. So I would memorize all the scriptures associated with the sermons first. And so I began.

I prayed for God to speak to my heart, and to guide me in my connection to His Word. I knew I didn't know the whole Bible and I knew that wasn't necessary to have understanding. Understanding, above all, I prayed for because it would change my life. I knew enough to know that Christianity was the way because Jesus was the Christ, the Son of God, by His sacrifice of His life in retribution for our sins. The church in D.C. taught me that from the beginning, there was no remission or forgiveness of sin without the shedding of blood.

Jesus had become the sacrificial lamb and came to earth to die for us. That was his whole purpose for coming here. And the history I had learned didn't tell me He was any blond-haired, blue-eyed Jesus. To the contrary, it told mine he had hair of lamb's wool and skin of copper. So Jesus had nappy hair and brown skin. That sounded like He was black to me. While I was here in New Jersey I would study all I brought with me and begin to work on a complete understanding. How could I pass it on, if I didn't have it myself?

My book is supposed to help many. And I remembered that God didn't take me that day in the mental hospital because I didn't want to go yet. Even though He spoke to my spirit that my life would be hard if I stayed, I wanted to stay and learn and give what my life would speak to the world, as God intended. I wondered sometimes how my mess of a life would ever bless or help anybody. But I had also learned that God had a way of using people who were humble and who thought themselves unworthy of the tasks that He gave them.

I would be in New Jersey for a year or so. When I went to visit Monie and her family a year later, I would not return to New Jersey. But I had studied the lessons from the church sermons and Bible studies from the church in D.C. as well as the sermons at the church in New Jersey over that year, and continued to learn at church and meditate on the Word at home. And I was transformed by what I learned. I had learned that it was necessary to learn the Word and meditate on the meaning that it spoke to me and I understood that what was transforming was keeping the Word in my mouth, my mind and my heart for God to work through.

In my late nights, my midnight hours, I began to see that God worked through His Word, causing me to gain understanding by connecting the Word, one part to another part based on the particular understanding I was seeking, and one day I woke up delivered from I was delivered from all of that which would keep me from God. I knew I was delivered because the spirit the Holy Spirit let me know that now I understood God's Word and His purpose. I had now experienced a complete transformation and was translated into the Kingdom of God. And once transformed I was free. The desire for anything that took me away from God was now just gone. God lifted it off of me. I knew in my spirit that it was gone. I knew it like I knew that my life would be hard if I stayed when I could go to him, when I didn't understand--it was spoken to my spirit inaudibly.

Suddenly, the taste for crack was just gone, and replaced with the desire to learn more and more about God and how to improve my relationship with Him, and be more like the Lord Jesus. I could not turn back because where God had now taken my spirit by His Word was so great that I could never return the lesser state where I was before I understood what I now understood through His Word; my life had taken new meaning and new direction. It was like learning to walk. Once one learned to walk, the need to crawl was gone forever. I could not speak the joy in my heart, because the realization was so immense and overwhelming. All I could do was cry.

I chose to keep allowing God teach me and I desired His teaching more than I desired those things I had used as a crutch to get me through. I could never trade the peace I now had, never trade knowing that He could not be visibly living in me when the devil's potion (crack) was in me. Crack hadn't been a part of my life for years then, and I would never go back. I knew if I ever slipped, it would never be able to hold me again because of what I now knew through His Word. I could not imagine not having God in my life again. I could not imagine not feeling His love again. It was the most incredible feeling I had ever had in my life, and it was better than any high I ever had to be close to God. Best of all, it was free.

To know that God had changed, transformed and delivered me by increasing my understanding and assuring me in my heart, my spirit and my soul that He is there, has always been there, and that He has always had the power to change me but needed me to see my life for what it was, and to choose Him over physical wants. He wanted me to see the difference in my spirit when I did the things that say that love Him, and then He just delivered me because I now understood how deliverance came to be (through understanding), so that I could appreciate deliverance and love Him just for being Him. I had to learn that exercising free will was an issue in my illness and that I couldn't get deliverance without understanding. Understanding just is or it is not. Partial understanding is not understanding. That is not to say that God cannot deliver without understanding, for there is nothing that God cannot do. Generally, though, understanding is a main ingredient to deliverance, and faith is the other. He is truly all-seeing and all-knowing. He certainly knew me better than I knew myself. I am quite overwhelmed every time I think about how He changed me in an instant. I was able to link the concepts from one part of the Word to the next and my picture was complete, and in that instance, my understanding was complete, and with that came my deliverance, like a flash. No bells and whistles, it just was. And if I had ten thousand tongues, I couldn't praise Him and thank Him enough. Hallelujah!

Chapter 18

I would end up staying at Monie's for more than a year. During that time I would reconnect with John and reestablish my connection with the same church that taught me so much. While I was still at Monie's, I had a minor stroke and was dragging my leg for a while, but was told that I should recover most of my functioning to normal levels. Months later, I would end up at my own house by working with Neta.

We had made an agreement that she changed, such that my rent was not covered in the way it was supposed to be, over the next few years. It was a 3-bedroom house and more room than I needed. Sheba ended up getting her own place when she returned from having the baby in Virginia. Before I got my place, I had actually left Monie's and stayed with Sheba for a while and took care of my beautiful granddaughter at Sheba's apartment while she worked. That was before C came back. I couldn't get away from his insulting, disrespectful, disgraceful, using, begging, worthless, lazy, trifling behind fast enough.

So when I got the house, I practically ran to it. I was fine for a year. Things started getting a little rough but manageable the next year. I had only worked with Neta since I had been there.

The job search was difficult. I had only had telemarketing jobs since I had been in the area, with exception of the two loan officer positions, and the mortgage market had crashed. I needed to find something in sales or marketing. Of course, I contacted John when I got back to the area and moved into the house a year ago and was back in church. I was still learning and hopeful about job prospects.

John told me about a job telemarketing for a remodeling company for homeowners. So I went and applied for that job and got it. It was part time but that would help me to have the funds for transportation to get to other jobs, so I took it. The job did what it was supposed to do, which was to supply me with "make it" money. That job closed my department after several months. I hadn't worked there long enough to get unemployment benefits. So I searched again for work.

My friend Mo called me one day wanting me to meet a man who owned his own company who wanted us to come into the business as shareholders. He worked in the same office as an energy products company. We met with others who also wanted to hear about the company. In order for me to buy my shares, I had to be employed. So, I sought and got a job with that company in business-to-business sales of energy rates and energy-saving products. I did well with that company. My hardest problem was getting to talk to the decision-maker or owner of the businesses. I remember my first commission check being in excess of $1600.

As it got hotter, the weather began to affect me more. But I kept at it. I was on mass transportation so I had to pace myself so I wouldn't overdo it. I continued to make money. My first client had somewhere around 10 locations, which was why my commission was so good. While I continued to make contact, not many others were as forthcoming as the first. I misunderstood some of the product information and passed misinformation on to a potential, and had a major mishap, and we didn't end up with that client I was totally embarrassed. I also had a mishap in putting on an outfit that I thought had been cleaned on another day not long after that. All that morning I thought that people I was around on the train and elevators, even in the office had underarm odor. When I discovered it was me, you could have bought me for a nickel. At the time I was the only female rep in a room full of men. I didn't go to the office for weeks. And I eventually let it go after I began to have a harder time getting contact with decision-makers on the phone. I was working full days but not bringing much in for a couple of months. I was spending more in transportation than I was bringing in.

Sheba and Nevaeh were living with me when I got my first commission. Little did I know, she had been letting C in the window of her room at night. When I discovered it after more than a month, I told him he would have to leave. After an argument with him trying once again to tell me what to do in my own house a few days later, I called the police. If it wasn't for my granddaughter I would have told them both to leave. I called the police and they didn't make him leave because the two of them said he had been staying there more than 30 days and that I would have to evict him through the courts.

I didn't have money for that. But I threatened to call the police again for a constructive eviction if they were not all gone in 30 days. They were gone in 30 days. My landlord knew C, and had put a clause in my lease that he was not to be on the premises. His living there would be grounds for eviction for me. So I did nothing but sweat for the next 30 days.

I breathed a sigh of relief when they were gone. I wondered why my daughter would go against me. But I knew that C had been working on her mind since day one, giving sob stories about his life, playing the victim. His relatives had told her what a bad seed he was, yet she still hoped he would change. I felt that was her motivation. No matter what, she struggled to make it with his behind.

He was my granddaughter's father. Sheba wanted a family--likely the family she never had because her father and I had not stayed together. Going to church helped me while they were there. A couple of times, C didn't let me take Nevaeh to church because, supposedly, he was a Muslim. He had none of the attributes of a Muslim and did not, from anything I saw exhibit any characteristics thereof. He didn't do anything and seemed to me a waste all round. He lived on women. Period.

He was a leech and I could not wait until my daughter would one day see and outgrow him. I would not' have her back' truly until she was rid of him and I knew that. But I would always be there for her no matter what he did or said. One day we would return to our relationship as mother and daughter. I knew that in my heart. I prayed for it. I just had to wait on the Lord to change her heart, for her own life.

Chapter 19

Things went bad at my house. I was unable to meet rent or utilities. My landlord moved one of her friends into the house so that some of the bills could be met and because she knew I had no place to go. We had tried some things to make money, but they didn't nearly cover the rent and eventually I went to my daughter's house. C wasn't there at the time. He was being a leech at someone else's house, but I felt in my heart that he would return. And he did.

He treated me disrespectfully as he always had. I went back to work for the remodeling company and got a room in a private home. He threw away my partials before I left. My work was only part time, so the weekly rent was hard, but I did it. I didn't go to church as regularly while I was there because it was a little difficult for John to get there and to church on time for Sunday School. After some months, my daughter called me wanting me to come back. C wasn't there often, but did come by sometimes. I couldn't understand for the life of me why she even dealt with him at all. But she had assured me that he was not coming back there to live. He had become physically abusive in front of Nevaeh and she was not going to have him in the house anymore. I praised God that she was finally waking up. She was also suing him for child support and got a restraining order because of the abuse. He was staying with another girl now. We tried to let her know what she was getting into while we could.

He would get his new girlfriend pregnant and she would come to court with him, obviously pregnant. I knew she was being given a sob story as though we had victimized him, because that's how we got suckered into helping him in the beginning: everybody had turned their backs on him and he didn't have a fair shake anywhere, according to him.

His new girlfriend would hear nothing we tried to tell her so she would not experience the same things that we did. I prayed that one day she would wake up as well, but for now he was the broke love of her life and was draining her. Sheba went on to get another job and I watched Nevaeh and picked her up and took her to school so Sheba could finally get ahead. I felt I owed it to her to be there for her. I had been absent at some crucial times in her life already. Eventually my job closed down again, having periods of slow down, so there was no strain for me to get there when I needed to be there for Nevaeh.

We are now together in the same dwelling and I have had all the time in the world to finish my testimony. I thank God for restoring our relationship. There is no C in my granddaughter's or my daughter's life anymore. Maybe when he wakes up, and if God wills it. I know that God does not call or draw all of us to Him, because all of us are not His children. He chooses us, not the other way around. So I pray for Nevaeh's sake that God draws C to Him, and that he hears the call, and changes his heart and his life. I also pray the same for anyone who is lost and does not know the one true God.

God is judging us all soon. Some, like those who worship idols or statues are being judged already because they have turned their faces away from God altogether.

I want to bless the world with what God has revealed to me to give back to the world: what He has placed on my heart. I believe I was born to give my story to the world; to go through what I went through in order to have my testimony, and to use my gift to give it to you. I believe that as much as I believe that Jesus was born to die for our sins. I pray that what is written here is pleasing in the sight of God, and that it speaks volumes to those who are caught up in an addicted world, and to those who don't know God or the Lord Jesus

Christ; that it even speaks to God's children whose understanding is incomplete. I pray that you all see and know that I was you. That I am you, transformed. And know that I am continuing to learn and be blessed every day. I hope that you see that you can be brought out of your condition, as well as I was. Know that God deals with us individuals and that your transformation will differ from mine, as our minds and spirits are individual. But the end result will be the same: You will be free.

I pray that the conclusion of this book will be a blessing to all, especially those who have walked the paths that I have, and I pray that it will change things in your hearts and minds. For those who do not know Jesus, I pray that it helps to get you to Him

IMAGINE
By Michelle Elaine

Imagine that God chose you,
Before the foundation of the world,
To be a direct participant in bringing about His Kingdom.
Imagine that He molded and shaped you and your life,
So that you would produce exactly what he intended that you produce,
Because of what He stored up in you.
Imagine that the part you play will bring a multitude to His feet.
Imagine that the world is changed forever by what you bring into it.
Are you imagining?
Can you imagine?
I don't have to.
And if you are a child of God,
Neither do you.

Insides Out, Part III, The Conclusion: THE LIGHT

Chapter 20 UNDERSTANDING

The Word of God says in Proverbs 4:7 "Wisdom is the principle thing, therefore get wisdom, and with all thy getting, get understanding." In fact, the whole of Proverbs 4 is about how finding understanding, then wisdom blesses you. The verse implies that understanding comes before wisdom. And it does. In order to get understanding one operates by studying, learning, and through his or her experiences, reaching a conclusion about how life is, and what is real. But that is just the surface.

Then there is the life after death question. Everybody makes a choice about God. Even if it is just that one decides not to believe in Him. Wisdom comes from the experience that comes as a result of operating within an understanding. I have found in studying the Word that the God-inspired Scriptures of the Holy Bible were written to put us on the correct path, yes, but were also written to mold us into the image that God intended, by the whole of experience having an effect upon each person and in each heart. Since the heart determines how we act, react, and feel, the heart is essentially who the person is. That's why God insists, in His Word, upon having your heart, the seat of your soul, the living essence of your spirit that lives forever, wherever it is after this physical life. And He will not receive us unto Himself after this physical life without it. Meanwhile He teaches and shows us grace and watches over us as we move and learn and make mistakes and get back up again, so that we come to know, and search for, and find Him.

I know that God creates us as babies in His image and gives each of us free will to choose. Physical life is necessary to bring the heart into full development, to full depth and maturity. Because death releases the fully developed heart which becomes the eternal soul.

With His Word we become acquainted with God, His nature, who He is, what He's done, and what He is going to do. And it is incumbent upon each of us to seek God's truth, and seek the answers to the questions in the recesses of our minds where God placed them. Common sense tells us that we are not the source. Neither is anything that we can measure, the source of itself. The source is God, from Whom all flows. And it is also true that God is the core of all things that are good. He is, and anything he says is, or will be. We need only sit back find the answers to the questions why. Finding the right answers to the questions 'why' leads to understanding. Why does the Lord require us to experience certain things? We should understand that God allows us to go through certain things because of what we will benefit from them spiritually, because of the knowledge and understanding which will be gained from the experience, and how the experience will grow the character that the person has. So the reason that God has us to experience certain things is to grow us, with the guidance of His Word, into understanding the answers to the questions in our hearts that need to be answered for peace in knowing that we know, that we know.

It's all in the Word and what God speaks to our hearts. That's how God works in individual lives to guide each person in his understanding. One should be terrified to leave this life without understanding: To close his eyes to an unknown. I know that one reason I'm still here is because I didn't understand. Once our eyes close for good, there is a final transformation into life or death. Everyone owes it to himself to seek the truth. Nothing ventured, nothing gained. I am sure that all who seek God and understanding will find them. (Matthew 7:7)

The most wonderful thing about His Word is that It does not return to Him void. He is the same yesterday, today and forever. The person who does not seek Him is lost. Period. Then there are those who sought Him and still don't have His clear truth. That happens because of misconceptions along the way. My little country church failed me by not being a good shepherd. The elders who taught Sunday school did not answer my questions and I wondered if they knew the answers to my questions back then. I doubted it.

The first understanding I had was in Islam. Islam educated me about the history of my people in this country: how we were stripped of our African history and heritage, and made ignorant, by denial of education, and beaten and coerced into submission, and made slaves. Islam taught me the things the government did since slavery to my people, and taught me the reasons we were in the condition that we were in as a people during the 1980's. I had never heard the information before and it rang true, so I believed that Islam was the whole truth. But I had based my belief on the wrong things. Just because the Muslims in this country were aware of specific details of our condition, that did not mean they held the whole spiritual truth. In fact I found that Islam did not speak to me in terms of the spiritual life, but in terms of the physical. Within it was unrest, and no peace. Jihad or Holy War, based upon Islamic principles, and following the prescribed Islamic order in prayer and in life were its focus. In living it, a spirit of rebellion existed in me because of my anger about the depth of the injustices committed against my people.

But there were no solutions about rising spiritually from the darkness and pain of my condition, not deliverance, not being translated into the Kingdom because of the acknowledgement of and belief in the sacrifice that Jesus made, not loving my neighbor as myself, not forgiving one another. I was just doing what I was supposed to do to fulfill the rites of Islam. Either you acted and did as a Muslim, or you were no longer Muslim. You are Christian from the time you accept Christ because you believe that Christ died for our sins, getting us back to God.

Before Jesus, everybody who died went to Hell, because everybody committed at least one sin, and sin cannot exist in the dwelling place of God. Jesus came here and lived and taught. In fact he came to be a sacrifice for our sins. When He died, he became the sacrificial Lamb, as there is no remission of sin without the shedding of blood. It would take the sacrifice of the Son to atone for so many sins for so many people. Without Jesus' sacrificing His life, we would all be in Hell because we sinned even once. The Qur'an came more than 600 years after the New Testament of the Holy Bible. And the last thing that the Holy Bible tells us is "Cursed is he who adds to or takes away from this book." (Rev. 22:18-19). The Qur'an is a separate book. Islam believes the Old Testament of the Bible, and doesn't accept the New Testament which teaches the life, death and resurrection of Jesus, the Christ, whose coming was foretold in the Old Testament.

Islam added its own book, and Islam took away the New Testament and its teachings, reducing Jesus to a prophet. The New Testament is not heard in Islam, but it is the basis of the Christian faith. We believe the entire Holy Bible. Why would God curse one who adds to or takes away from His Word? Because doing so would change what He said. And who in the "annals of all history" fulfills the picture of the Son of God, but Jesus? The Word of God is fulfilled in Jesus. Nothing else completes our understanding 360 degrees, but Him. What is marvelous is that once we accept Jesus, we can never be snatched from God's hand, no matter what. And "no one cometh unto the Father except by Me (Jesus)". One who acknowledges that there is a greater power than himself or the leaders of this world, owes it to himself to learn about Jesus, because he can acknowledge God all day, but if he denies the blood of Christ, he will never see God or enter into His Kingdom. Accepting and believing in the Son, Jesus is our only way into God's Kingdom. I do not know love like God does and I am still learning, but I can imagine how great God's pain was as He watched His Son, knowing what His Son's sacrifice was for, yet knowing that the innocent, Jesus, must endure His full wrath to save us from certain eternal death. Only an innocent could be a reasonable sacrifice. And how blasphemous non-believers must have been in God's eyes. And one can never be a part of a Kingdom where Christ's church is, if in his heart he does not believe. Study so that you learn to understand and are "approved of God, a worker who does not need to be ashamed, rightly dividing the Word of Truth". God's highest commands are these: First, "You shall love the

Lord thy God, with all thy heart, all thy mind, all thy soul and all thy strength. The second one, like it, that you shall love thy neighbor as thy self."(Luke 10:27) Understanding how obeying these highest commandments affect the soul explains why it is important that we do obey them: Obeying them changes the human heart into a Godly heart, led by the Word.

"Oh, taste and see that the Lord is good".

Chapter 21 - How Do We Get to God

In John 14:6, Jesus says "I am the way, the truth and the life. No one comes to the Father (God) except by Me." The example of Jesus' life from His humble birth "wrapped in swaddling clothes (or rags) and born in a manger (or feeding trough)" first says to us how little God is concerned with wealth. God allowed His Son to be born to very humble parents who knew who He was before He got here. The teachers that I had in Islam intimated that for Jesus to be conceived, that God would have to have performed the sinful act of intercourse with Mary, as that is the physical way to reproduce. But Mary knew and Joseph knew through direct word from God through His angels that the child in Mary was conceived of the Holy Spirit. That God the Spirit need only say "be and it is" or kun faya kun, the Islamic equivalent. John, the Baptist, leapt in his mother, Elisabeth's womb when Mary went to visit her, because John the Baptist knew while in his mother's womb that Jesus was there.

Jesus came to die for us; to provide the way for us to get back to God. And sin has to be atoned for in order to become free from sin in death. Jesus became the sacrificial Lamb. He was a teacher of the Word atoning for sin. And He taught us how to act, how to treat one another, what was important to God and how to please God. Before

Jesus, when you died, if you committed a single sin you could not enter into the Kingdom of God and went to Hell, as God does not look upon sin, nor can sin be in His dwelling place. Jesus provided the way through His teachings from when He walked the earth.

The truth of His teachings is obvious. When one begins to live the life that Jesus set forth in His teachings, he or she transforms from death into eternal life in the hereafter. We are also blessed with learning about the nature of the love of God for us that "He gave his only begotten Son, that whosoever believeth in Him shall not perish, but have everlasting life." (John 3:16) The Lord Jesus also tells us exactly who will be saved, and lets us know His conditions for saving us. It has nothing to do with what a person has, but again, with his heart. "If you believe in you heart and confess with your mouth that Jesus died for your sins and was raised from the dead, you shall be saved". (Romans 10:9) Now there is no way to believe something in your heart unless you, study it and come to understand it; to know it. So the Lord wants us to hear and learn about Him and make the decision to follow Him, based on believing what we have and heard being taught, so that we can become a part of the fold and be taught that there is good news. That's why people go to church and I am proud to say that today's Baptist church, teaches the living Word of God. That is because they must now go to seminary school before leading from the pulpit, thank God. Now I recommend the Baptist church. I would also recommend that if you have not begun attending church to learn about the Lord, His life and the way you should live, that you should begin now. And don't worry that you don't know everything. The church has the responsibility to teach you, so that you live spiritual lives on earth, and to prepare you for the eternal hereafter. You only need to confess with your mouth and believe in your heart that Jesus died for our sins and was raised from the dead on the third day (which saves your soul), and the church teaches you the rest. Tomorrow is not promised to any of us. When you are saved, it is at the moment that you decide to follow and learn about Christ. God has provided the church, so that we can learn and get understanding. That is what church is for.

The church is necessary for your full transformation to take place. Just reading the Word of God is good, but for understanding and clarification, the church is where to go. There are the Saints of God, one of which you will become when your understanding is complete. Does that mean you will be sinless or that the Saints of God are sinless? No. We still live in our flesh and we commit sins every day. We never arrive at perfection: because we are flawed, and not without sin. What is different is the heart, mind, soul. Also, there is now forgiveness of sin that we receive when we ask for it, rather than atonement for sin. Jesus' sacrifice has already atoned for all sin. And our strength comes from God, not ourselves. So we rely on God, and every word that comes from His mouth (Matthew 4:4) "Lean not on your own understanding, but in all thy ways acknowledge Him, and He will direct your path."(Proverbs 3:5-6) So we should not accept understandings that are separate from Him, the source, for that is how we become mislead in understanding.

So go to church with your questions, find answers, get understanding and peace. Learn about the gifts God has given you. Learn what it is to know Jesus and to learn His way, His truth and His light and be with people whose aim is to live their lives in His likeness, having been transformed.

It is the duty of every Christian to bring others to the faith, by spreading the gospel, which, simply is the good news that, "For God so loved the world that He gave His only begotten Son, that whosoever believes in Him shall not perish, but have everlasting life." (John 3:16) And know that" without faith, it is impossible to please God, because anyone who comes to Him must believe that He exists and that he rewards those who earnestly seek Him," (Hebrews 11:6)

Chapter 22: KNOWING GOD

First thing, no one can ever be "good" to the point of becoming God. Nor can being "good" get you into the Kingdom of God, for it is not by works that you get there. If you doubt the first statement, then, go back for a second and think: what source are you of all life? Are you the system that makes things grow of your own substance or power? Can you make a baby develop and give it a soul? If you doubt the second statement, know that "it is by grace that you have been saved, through faith—and this is not from yourselves, it is the gift of God, not by your works, that no one may boast" (Ehesians 2:8-9) Second thing: it is not all about you. God's agenda is a Holy one. It is higher than ours. Our thoughts are not the same as His. His are higher. (Isaiah 55:9) And what He is transforming us for besides eternal life is only known to Him. And think about it. If you are not a part of God's plan, whose plan are you a part of? You know. I don't have to tell you. There are only two sides.

When you learn about God, "I" goes out the window, as you realize that the focus is on all of creation and your place in it, not on what you think and how things are in your head, but of what God wants and what God says. I know that there is life outside the physical body because He said it and because He briefly showed me that it is, when I was lost.

It is our job in life to learn and see that our purpose is to follow the instructions sent forth by the Word of God, to obey His Law so we can be molded into His likeness. He gives us all gifts to use in the body of the church so that we can use them to bring others to the fold to be given understanding and edification, which is our other job. The Lord doesn't want us to fail to be in the church because of the additional gain we get spiritually by learning what He says through another person in that fold who is operating in his gift from God.

The beauty of following Jesus and obeying God is that it is natural. It takes away questions and doubt and blossoms the heart, mind and soul. The more one understands the more the Lord reveals to him, and the closer to Him and His way he gets. And the more God can find ways to use him in His service. It is not instead a drudgery of conformance, but a joy and pleasure to serve the Lord with gladness, knowing that what you are doing feels good and is so pleasing in the sight of the Lord; that he is using you and your gift. When one is a blessing to others, God is pleased. But it is impossible to get there without learning God's transforming Word. Prayer is an essential. It is direct communication with God. God loves His Word because it is the truth. When speaking to God we need to speak His word. His Word says "You have not because you ask not, or you ask amiss."(James 4:2-3) That means you can miss the answers to your prayers because you don't ask in the right way. God always knows what is in your heart better than you do. He wants to bless us with the things we want, but he wants us to have clean motives for our wants, and not want for selfish reasons, but to serve, whenever possible. So it is good to use His Word in prayer. God delivers, blesses. For example, I may need a car and I want to pray for one because soon I won't be able to have the mobility I need without it.

I might start my prayer with Mark 11:26-27 "Father God, you said in your Word that whoever says to this mountain (or big problem) be thou removed and cast into the sea, and does not doubt in his heart, but believes these things he says shall be done, he shall have whatever he says". Therefore, I am asking that You provide me with a car, Lord because you know that I need one, and there are things I know you want me to do, and You know the bus and train will not allow me to do all that I am called to do. I humbly ask you with a clean heart to show me the path to follow to get it or just provide it, Lord as only you can...". That is just an example.

The Word has to be internalized to be effective. The more His Word is meditated upon, the more it becomes a part of you. Just as in the beginning of this book, I kept repeating the laws of "my philosophy," now I repeat the Word of God in my mind and visualize what it says, which helps me to memorize it more readily. Then He sows it into my heart.

Memorizing and meditating on the Word does not just help in prayer, it helps you live as God wants you to, and He blesses those who are acquainted with His Word because it is also His Will for us. (Psalms 1:1-4)" Blessed is the man who walks not in the counsel of the ungodly, nor stands in the path of sinners, nor sits in the seat of the scornful, But his delight is in the law of the Lord, and in His law he meditates day and night. He shall be like a tree planted by rivers of water, that brings forth its fruit in its season, whose leaf shall not wither and whatever he does shall prosper." What a blessing! That's a blessing just for meditating on His Word and doing His Will. Why? Because meditating on His word causes the understanding that transforms. 'Whatever you do shall prosper'. God's Word is amazing and eternal. It provides for everything in any walk of life, and if we do His Will, there are countless blessings in store for us. Meditating on His Word and applying it to prayer and speaking the Word to problems changes things and increases faith and causes us to walk in the way that is pleasing to God. God doesn't expect any of us to be perfect and not to sin at all. If He did, He would have made us angels because they don't have free will.

The nature of God is of a watchful, caring father who loves us unconditionally, and the gift through Jesus' life, death and resurrection, is that forgiveness without blood sacrifice is available because Jesus sacrificed His life already and those who believe in Him will benefit, and one day return to God the Father. He will chastise us and allow us to go through whatever it takes to get us back to Him if we stray. He knows what it takes for each of us. And everybody's journey is as individual as people are different. He knew us all before the foundation of the world, down to the number of hairs on each of our heads.(Luke 12:7) He created us. Our mothers merely birthed us. And God has had a plan for each of us since the beginning. He knew everything would happen that happened in the Bible and made a plan to bring His creation back to Him after sin seeped into our relationship with Him.

God is the source. He is pure goodness and wisdom. He always was, is, and will always be. Yet He has never changed and is the same yesterday, today and forever.

Chapter 23 - DELIVERANCE

When I started out in Part 1, my focus was on me and my idea of what I needed. It was about finding a path for myself and others by way of some truth that I would discover, which would be so profound that it would change the world and its ways. But because the truth was sought without regard to or without acknowledgement of the shed blood of Jesus, and was about being recognized, it was likely self-serving in the eyes of God. What I thought was a completed revelation of truth was only the beginning of my journey, and life would teach me that. God could not give me the truth then. If He gave me the truth then, I would not have recognized it, because I lacked necessary understanding to receive it.

Once I fully understood the path to God and got on it, I did the things that God would have me do to grow in Him. As I grew, I came to understand why I should be on this particular path and the benefits of being on the path, as God planned. I came to know Jesus and His love for us, that was so great that He would lay down His life for us, so that we would not perish in death, but have the opportunity to enter into Heaven. I could never see the truth without seeing Jesus, because Jesus is a huge part of it. It would never make common sense without Him. Once I understood, and received Jesus and studied God's Word, I found that everything now made perfect sense, and I realized I had found the truth. And I submitted myself to God, and to the Lord, Jesus Christ. From that point the Lord has led me and increased in my heart and He used His people to teach me what I needed to know about the Word. By understanding the Word and what God has done to accomplish the purpose for which He sent his Word, I was able to be molded and God stepped in and removed my addiction. Crack had been a God before God in my life. The more I stayed in the Word, the more I came to dislike crack more than I liked it, and eventually I detested it and put it down for good.

God removed the desire and craving for crack and the dreams that I used to have about using, after periods of time not using. Even when I slipped and tried it, I still put it down again because I was not going to throw my blessing away, and because crack was no longer remotely attractive to me anymore. I was walking now, no longer crawling. Besides, I just did not want the feeling anymore, or the hiding it, or what it did to my life and my relationships. It had devastated my life and took everything with it, including my self-respect and my morals. Worst of all, crack kept me from God: I wouldn't want to have any relationship with God when I was using, and using caused me to have a great shame, that I wouldn't have in my life now.

Anything that kept me away from God, I learned, was something that I could no longer have in my life, if I was to grow in God. So crack had to be put away so that I could "hear". Naturally and without any assistance from anyone but the Lord, it was put away and I was now "a new creature and old things had passed away, behold, all things were new" (2 Corinthinans 5:17).

Very simply the Lord delivered me, as only He can, and restored my life while I was yet still on earth. I knew that my eternal soul was at stake and I had to change in order to live forever in the right place. And he delivered me because I pursued him and wanted Him more than anything else. But He would not have done it if I was not willing to let the drug go. He doesn't force us to do anything. We have to choose on our own. That is why we have free will. I learned that one is surely dead, while still living if he uses crack, because that is the only substance that I have ever known that has the ability to take control of a person's soul, taking all reverence and regard towards God, causing a person to seek it at all costs. The Lord yanked away my greatest shame and removed it from my life in an instance of growth in Him. Some things Jesus just does for us because He loves us. When you grow enough in the Lord, a demon like that cannot continue to live in you because the Spirit of God and a demon like crack cannot dwell in the same place for long. It will be cast out, naturally. All you have to do is meditate on the Word of God, which is your sword and keep His Word in your mouth. He knows that we can't do some things by ourselves, but if we want it, and trust and believe that He will 'move our mountains', He will. What we can't do on our own, we can do through Him. "I can do all things through Christ, who strengthens me."(Phillipians 4:13) Christ is a healer. We need only to BELIEVE it.

Chapter 24 - TRUSTING GOD

Trusting God is likely the hardest thing for a person to do who is new to Christianity. What it means to trust God is being able to let things go and give them to God to handle and to wait on His move or His hand to take care of them. Trusting God is impossible without faith and belief in Him and what He said. One has to be more than acquainted with God in order to be able to trust Him wholeheartedly, because trust, like faith comes by hearing or understanding and understanding (hearing) comes by the Word of God.(Romans 10:17)

Trust in God also comes from knowing who God is, what he expects, and what He is able to do. In fact, trust in God allows Him to operate fully within us and in our lives, and give us what we desire. What we desire changes as we grow in Him. The Word tells us to "Delight yourself in the Lord, and he will give you the desires of your heart."(Psalms 37:4) Our delight in the Lord is automatic when we understand that the joy or delight is in knowing Him, His plan and our place in it; it is an irreplaceable joy that gives us direction and peace.

There is a place in our learning that we arrive at understanding God and what He wants. When we get there, we love Him even more because we see His plan and how he planned from the beginning to lead us back to Him with fully developed and changed hearts. That He loves us unconditionally and He has done and He will do for us so that we learn, understand and achieve His purpose in us, and, thereby, do our part in carrying out His plan.

Many Christians love God, but do not fully trust Him even though we think we do. We will pray a prayer and ask God to do something. If God doesn't work it out in the time that we think that He should, we sometimes take back the problem and try to work it out for ourselves. That means we don't trust Him and we begin to think that we have to do something about the problem, or we become worried, which shows a lack of faith and trust. Whenever we give a problem or situation to God, we must stand back and allow Him do what we have asked. If we trust Him and His Word, we can be assured that when we ask God for things that are in His will for us, He gives them to us. He wants us to be prosperous and He wants us to do what He wills. God is supernatural and will work in our lives and do all things in supernatural ways that neither we nor anyone else can explain, because He is the source and is not limited to any sphere of understanding, reasoning, realm or knowledge that we have. The Word does say that "faith without works is dead" (James 2:17), which means that we should do all that we can in a given situation, so that God has something to work through. Then we give it to God to work it out as only He can. And remember that nothing that we accomplish is by our might, but by His will or by His help. Without Him we can do nothing; He gives us our very breath to be able to even move.

We must trust Him in order to see His glory in our lives; to see the miracles He wants to show us, so that we can give Him the glory, honor and praise He deserves, being our only refuge and strength in situations that we are unable to surmount. He creates testimony in us when He delivers us from problems or makes a way out of no way. He is our protection from dangers seen and unseen. Children of God understand that "No weapon formed against us shall prosper, and every tongue which rises against us in judgement, we shall condemn. This is the heritage of the servants of the Lord, and our righteousness is from God" (Isaiah 54:17)

Our trust is built on our knowledge and understanding of Him and is activated by faith. So when we give something to God, we need to leave it there, trusting Him, having done all we can, and just stand on and trust in Him. "And having done all (that you can) to stand. Stand, therefore, with your loins girt about with truth, and having on the breastplate of righteousness, and your feet shod with the preparation of the gospel of peace. Above all, take the shield of faith, wherewith you shall be able to quench all the fiery darts of the wicked. And take the helmet of salvation and the sword of the spirit, which is the word of God. Praying always, with all prayer and supplication in the Spirit..." (Ephesians 6:14-19).

Finally, we must wait for the Lord to show up with our solutions for everything we have given to Him to solve. And we must not be "anxious about anything, but in EVERY situation, by prayer and petition, and with thanksgiving, present our requests to God. Then the peace of God that passes all understanding will keep our hearts and minds through Christ Jesus. (Philippians 4:6-7) And remember that "those who wait upon the Lord shall renew their strength. They shall mount up with wings like eagles, they shall run and not grow weary, and they shall walk and not grow faint." (Isaiah 40:31) In other words, we will be able to withstand by the renewal of our strength by way of our trust in the Lord.

Trust Him and watch Him move in your life. Know that He is our protection. There is spiritual warfare going on in all of us. He is the voice of good when we are tempted. We all sin, but the more we listen to His voice, the less we are tempted. We do "not fight against flesh and blood but against the rulers of darkness of this world and against spiritual wickedness in high places". (Ephesians 6:12) God provides us with a way in all cases. We are more than conquerors, through Christ. Former condemnation is no more for those who know and love Christ. (Romans 12:1) He will automatically cause all things to work together for the good of those who love Him and are called to His purpose. (Romans 8:28) If you are a Christian, you have been drawn to the faith by God. You do not choose Him, He chooses you. And if you ask Him for what you need in Jesus' name, He will do it.(John 15:16) If you have been drawn, rest assured that God intends to work through you in some way, and through gifts that He has given you that you may not even know that you have. Go into the fellowship of the church, that is headed by Christ and He will draw out what you are here to do. Look for it. It may be big or small in your eyes, but in God's eyes we all put ingredients into His purpose being fulfilled. Count it all joy what God gives you to do and know that He's 'got you' because you are His child, even more than an earthly parent: He's 'got you' on things you don't even see coming. Trust Him.

Chapter 25 - INTERPRETING MY SIGNS FROM GOD

Back in Part 1, God showed me some signs. The first sign that convinced me that He existed was the 3 circles in a row in the clouds in the sky. I interpret them to mean that God was showing me that He is a triune God. The trinity is the "us" in "Let us make mankind in our image.." (Genesis 1:26). And the circle, by design has no beginning or ending.

The second sign was the voice at my Aunt Stella's apartment door that said "Which one of you is that?" That was an indicator for me that God was listening and was there with me, even though I was lost in confusion and not acknowledging Jesus. I had accepted Jesus that day in church in the country, and just like the Word says in John 10:29 "My Father, who has given them to me, is greater than all; no one can snatch them out of My Father's hand." He was still with me, still watching over me even in the state that I was in and actually spoke to me, asking a question of me in a strong male voice. Who else but God would know what was going on inside my head in order to ask that question? He was with me, guiding me.

The 3rd was the radio that didn't work that played and announced a party in my honor. That, I believe was a foretelling of a future event that is now closer than ever.

The 4th was leaving my body. When I saw a body on the floor, yet I still had a body, I realized that there was life after death. I determined that I was not finished and that I wanted to tell the story of my life. So I was returned to the body and the Spirit of God in me let me know that my life would be difficult if I stayed and I decided to stay anyway. Now I understand that my life had to be difficult in order to grow my testimony, and give people a story to help them in life.

The 5th was the women at the sanitarium who looked as though they were dying. They looked hollow as though they had been drained of life. I knew I was supposed to help them in some way. They had not looked like that when I was outside of the room. There was a reason that God had pointed them out to me. Now I realize that He was showing me that there would come a day that I would be one of them, as I remembered seeing myself in the mirror, looking as though I had died. They were the hollow souls of the addicted and I would become one of them. They are a large part of the reason that it is necessary that this book be published.

6th there was the day before I went into the zoo that my friend's daughter, Teresa was a toddler on the bed. It seemed that she was lifted up and turned over to face me, with nothing touching the bed but her hand. She had a smile on her face. That told me that there was an invisible presence there. Perhaps it was an angel, as we believed when Adrian fell off the top bunk in slow motion. Teresa was not afraid, so I knew the presence was good—and of God. That meant that there was nothing to fear and my experience would be good. God would be there.

Then, 7th, the second time I went through my experience, there were the pulleys in the pit. God let me know He was there and would be speaking to me because he let one pulley move and one would not move. I knew ahead of time which would move and which would not. He let me know that I was hearing His voice, that He was leading me.

The 8th, were the tigers in the pit kept going from 0 degrees to 90 degrees. Neither tiger went all the way to the other side completing the whole walk of 180 degrees of the semi-circle. I now believe that was an indication that I didn't have the whole story about God and He would show me. It also meant that possibly I would keep getting halfway to understanding because my addiction would keep turning me back the wrong way.

The 9th were the birds in the zoo. The first had its beak stuck in its own back and the second stood naturally. That signified putting one's old man to death and becoming a new creature in Christ, after understanding of the Word of God transforms. The fact that they were trimmed in gold let me know that this sign was significant and valuable in my life. And it is.

Then, 10th there was the elephant in the barn. I believed He showed me the elephant, since it is said that the elephant never forgets. This was His way of telling me to never forget my experience. He caused me to record the story, registering a copyright, thinking I would be publishing it, but it would be decades before the whole story would be ready. After sending Part One to about 20 publishers, I suddenly knew in my Spirit that I wouldn't be publishing the book for years, until I had lived long enough to answer the questions in the book myself, and that my experience had not reached a point of fruition. It has now been 30 years and my understanding is now complete. And I am a child of God, saved by the sacrifice of Jesus Christ, His shed blood in remission of my sins and the remission of the sins of all who follow Him. My story will now bear fruit.

11th, God identified my enemy. The old white man was literal and symbolic. He was the ideals of the past; the prejudice, the discrimination, inequality, and hatred against my people. God was letting me know that the old white man is still here, but mostly a dying breed, He is very old. Someday soon, he would die, or be made inconsequential--impotent, so that his children will be free to receive light from one whose body is clothed in the skin his father hates.

The pinwheel earrings were 12th, given to me by the staff on Nicols 6. They showed me that the staff also saw the pinwheel of light that God used to speak to me. At the time, the light simply calmed me. Now I believed that it was God speaking things to my spirit that I would come to understand in the future. I think they were the staff of Nicols 6's way of telling me that they knew that I wasn't crazy. They, too, saw the light. One day I would write the book and others would see the light that I saw.

There is a circular design to life: that what you sow you reap, that God is the same, yesterday, today, and forever, that God is Alpha and Omega, the beginning and the ending, that understanding, true understanding leads from a point and is all-encompassing in its elements, logically returning to its initial point. One who still has questions still has understanding to get. Answering your questions removes doubt. If you believe and do not doubt, there is no limit to what God can do in your life.

Chapter 26 - WHO AM I?

I am what God made me to be. I am God's child saved by the shed blood of Jesus Christ, which I acknowledge, receive, and accept in my heart and spirit. It is my responsibility to pass on to others what He has revealed to me through my experiences, that others may also benefit.

I know that God reveals to all of His children those things that transform them through knowing His Word. I am a living example of the power of God to affect change because of what He did in my life: I am a living testimony of the power of God and His ability to completely change the lives of those who seek Him.

I am a new heart, a new soul and a new mind in Him who is the Lord of my life. Since I was willing to submit to His will, He was able to mold me. And in as much as I am receptive, He is willing to breathe life into me and allow me to feel His presence, and I am able to sup with Him, and He with me. I am fully able to see what He continues to do in me, that I may give it to you in hopes that you fully receive from Him through me. I have completely sold out to God and whatever He would have me do. I am tuned into His voice and have completely sacrificed my mind, soul, and body to Him, that He may use me as He sees fit.

Therefore, I am a living sacrifice, usable by God, which is my reasonable service to Him. Even so, my sacrifice does not compare to the sacrifice of Jesus. And I would lay down my life rather than deny Him. I am a child of God, obedient to His will, knowing nothing can separate me from His love, "neither death nor life, neither angels nor demons, nor height nor depth, nor things present nor things present nor things to come, nor any other created thing shall be able to separate us from the love of God, which is in Christ Jesus, our Lord." (Romans 8:38-39)

And no, I am not perfect, but I am striving toward perfection; as I am still in the flesh, and I still have the sin nature, and I do sin. But my heart is in the right place; to do the will of God and walk in His likeness to the best of my ability, and that's good enough for Him. I love the Lord, with all my heart, all my mind, all my soul and all my strength. And I love my neighbor like I love myself. (Mark 12:30-31)

My given name is Michelle Elaine. Michelle means god-like and Elaine means light. So my name means god-like light. I will be trying to live up to the name for the remainder of my life. I will try my best, always to be a reflection of who God's Word has transformed me into, or what I know in my heart that He wants me to be, to show Him a measure of my love for Him, and for my gratitude for His mercy, His Grace, His love, and His compassions that are new every morning. AMEN!

WHEN I FINISHED IT

When I finished it, I felt the weight of the world lift off of me.
Mama had told me years ago, before I started it, that I had to stop carrying the weight of the world on my shoulders.
So, it was in my heart long before my quest, which started it.
When I finished it, I had managed, through Christ, to conquer the way of life that deceived me,
And it is now under my feet.
When I finished it, I had conquered, through Christ, the substance of the beast of ignorance and shame,
And it is now under my feet.

Before I finished it, the substance of the beast had taken my direction, my spirit, my self-respect.
And when I lost my son, at the tender and innocent age of 12, I thought I would perish before I finished it.
I felt that I was in a flood of problems and circumstances
But then God stepped in and covered me with His light and love, before I finished it.
And before I finished it, He gave me understanding to give others, who don't know Him,
And to show others being controlled that they can shed the substance of the beast that plagues them.
Before I finished it, my heart was that they should know Jesus and what He did.
When I finished it, I think I got the point across,
And helped at least some of the lost to see the Way, so that they may, too, be transformed,
And have their testimony.
When I finished it, I knew God was the true author, writing with me the whole time.
When I finished it, I praised Him.
When I finished it, I gave Him all the glory and honor.
Now that it is finished, I feel that this is my third child that I carried for decades, finally delivered.
Now that it is finished, I pray that it breathes new light and life into those who choose to hear it.

-Michelle Elaine